Masterclass: Developing Characters

Irving Weinman

First published in Great Britain in 2014 by John Murray Learning. An Hachette UK company.

First published in US in 2014 by The McGraw-Hill Companies, Inc.

Copyright © Irving Weinman 2014

The right of Irving Weinman to be identified as the Author of the Work has been asserted by him in accordance with the Copyright, Designs and Patents Act 1988.

Database right Hodder & Stoughton (makers)

The *Teach Yourself* name is a registered trademark of Hachette UK.

British Library Cataloguing in Publication Data: a catalogue record for this title is available from the British Library.

Library of Congress Catalog Card Number: on file.

Paperback ISBN 978 1 471 80446 5

eBook ISBN 978 1 471 80448 9

10 9 8 7 6 5 4 3 2 1

The publisher has used its best endeavours to ensure that any website addresses referred to in this book are correct and active at the time of going to press. However, the publisher and the author have no responsibility for the websites and can make no guarantee that a site will remain live or that the content will remain relevant, decent or appropriate.

The publisher has made every effort to mark as such all words which it believes to be trademarks. The publisher should also like to make it clear that the presence of a word in the book, whether marked or unmarked, in no way affects its legal status as a trademark.

Every reasonable effort has been made by the publisher to trace the copyright holders of material in this book. Any errors or omissions should be notified in writing to the publisher, who will endeavour to rectify the situation for any reprints and future editions.

Typeset by Cenveo® Publisher Services.

Printed and bound in Great Britain by CPI Group (UK) Ltd, Croydon CR0 4YY.

John Murray Learning policy is to use papers that are natural, renewable and recyclable products and made from wood grown in sustainable forests. The logging and manufacturing processes are expected to conform to the environmental regulations of the country of origin.

John Murray Learning
338 Euston Road
London NW1 3BH

www.hodder.co.uk

Also available in ebook

To all my writer friends and especially,
as always, to Judith

Acknowledgements

Thanks first to Sam Richardson of John Murray Learning for putting this my way, then to Victoria Roddam of John Murray Learning for working hard and structuring the project and getting it accepted. And many thanks to Jamie Joseph, also at John Murray Learning, for his support, encouragement and quick, sensible decisions.

The author and publisher would like to express their thanks to the authors extracts of whose work appear in this book. These are listed in the References section.

Contents

	About the author	vi
	Introduction	vii
1	Sources of character	1
2	General character types: flat	14
3	General character types: rounded	32
4	Narration and character	56
5	Showing character through action	82
6	Showing character through dialogue	106
7	Character: symbolism and satire	133
8	Character: voice and turning point	154
	References	178
	Index	181

About the author

Among Irving Weinman's critically acclaimed novels are Tailor's Dummy, Virgil's Ghost, Stealing Home *and his latest,* Wolf Tones. *He has taught fiction writing in the United States and England, most recently a masterclass for the MA in Creative Writing and Authorship at Sussex University. He was founder-director of the Key West Writers' Workshop and a director of the Key West Literary Seminar. Irving Weinman lives in East Sussex with his wife, the poet Judith Kazantzis.*

Introduction

At the first meeting of every fiction writing course I teach – from absolute beginners to published writers or postgraduates – I say the same thing: 'This is my short lecture on how to write and how not to write. It's my best lecture.'

Then I say, 'This is the first part of the lecture – how to write.' I take a pen and for a few seconds I write on a piece of paper. Then I pick up the piece of paper and say, 'It says, "This is how to write."'

After a pause (I'm hamming it up, I know), I say, 'This is the second part of the lecture – how not to write.' I pick up my pen, take a fresh sheet of paper, look down at it, scratch my head and look away from the paper. I look up at the ceiling. I purse my lips and furrow my forehead. I tilt back my head and narrow my eyes, looking straight up at the ceiling. I make noises, ums and aahs of effort. Again, I scratch my head. Then I hold up the still-blank piece of paper to the group and say, 'This is how not to write.' I add something about inspiration or the muse not coming at my command, coming only, if at all, when I'm actually writing.

'That's it,' I say, 'end of lecture.'

The entire performance has taken about four or five minutes. Then I add, 'Whatever else happens in this course, this is the best advice you'll get from me.'

It's true. You learn to write by writing. You learn to write fiction by writing. And you learn to write and develop characters by writing. Yes, I certainly want you to read the rest of this book, but this is the single most important piece of advice that I can give you.

The masterclass concept

This book follows as closely as possible the format of a live creative writing masterclass. There, students read out a piece of work, having distributed copies to everyone else, including the writer giving the masterclass who hasn't seen this work before. Following this, the writer gives her/his response, explaining what is good and what could usefully be worked on. Though a bit of time is given to the response of other students, most of the comment is the writer–leader's response. In this book, the 'pieces of work' are extracts from published fiction I've chosen to illustrate important concepts in the development of character. The examples are necessarily of good writing, that is, writing that achieves good character development.

Various short and mid-length writing exercises focus the reader on practical writing work related to each chapter's topic. These are as follows.

 Snapshot is a short exercise of about 250 words.

 Write is an exercise of about 750 words.

 Edit is a reworking of a previous piece or exercise.

There are two other features within each chapter:

 Key ideas distil the most important points and ideas.

 Focus points at the end of each chapter will help you hone in that chapter's core messages.

THE WORKSHOP

Each of the book's main chapters ends with a workshop. The workshop is an important series of questions about your own fiction writing linked to the topic(s) of that chapter. The idea is to have you think about your writing as if these were questions raised by your fellow students and/or workshop leader in an actual group setting. Sometimes the workshop will include editing a piece of your fiction arising from the questions, as would be the case after a group workshop session.

Who this book is for

Books on creative writing are aimed either at a general or specific audience. The general audience is anyone interested, from beginners to more advanced writers, those with a substantial practice of creative writing. This book is for more advanced writers of fiction.

The basic assumption of this book is that you are someone with a substantial portfolio of fiction. This could be a number of short stories, a novel or a major part of a novel, or a number of works of fiction in progress. Behind this assumption are two others: that you really like fiction and have read a good amount of it.

Since, among other writing exercises, you'll be working with your own existing fiction, the assumption of your fiction portfolio – your body of existing work – is of practical importance. Another important assumption of your experience with writing fiction is that you have an understanding of the basic terms related to working with fiction. This includes structural terms relating to plot as well as terms of presentation relating to narration. It also includes an understanding of terms relating to language and grammar. Because of these assumptions, this book doesn't define these terms; nor is there a glossary. If you're unsure about any of the terms, it's easy to find them explained in books or on the Internet.

1

Sources of character

What is character in fiction? The short answer: everything. The fiction we read is presented by and through its characters. Even a story without people, say about elephants or extraterrestrials, is still about characters because fiction is written by people for other people to read. Fiction happens by and through beings to whom human readers respond with human understanding and human emotions. Character is so deeply integral to fiction that it's often assumed in discussions of fiction rather than explicitly presented.

Character is at the heart of fiction. This means:

- The reader connects with fiction through its characters.
- What happens in fiction – the story and plot – is presented through characters.
- What a work of fiction means – the theme – is revealed by what happens to the characters.

Write for ten minutes

Write a one- or two-page start of a piece of fiction (300–500 words)
in which no character is present. You can describe a scene, a
place, or setting. Write in the third person. Take no more than
ten minutes to write this. Then leave it for ten minutes and read it
over. Explain to yourself what is has to do with character.

What is character?

Look at the opening chapter of Thomas Hardy's novel **The Return
of the Native** (1878). Hardy labels all the chapter headings. The
second chapter is labelled, 'Humanity appears on the scene.' In other
words, only in the second chapter does a character appear; the first
chapter, it would seem, is devoid of character. Here is its opening:

Chapter 1
A face on which time makes but little impression

> *A Saturday afternoon in November was approaching the
> time of twilight, and the vast tract of unenclosed wild
> known as Egdon Heath embrowned itself moment by
> moment. Overhead the hollow stretch of whitish cloud
> shutting out the sky was as a tent which had the whole
> heath for its floor.*

From the very start, the chapter label in referring to the landscape
as 'A face' brings in a human characteristic. Naming the day, the
time of day, and the month refers to human culture. And the simile
ending the second sentence brings human scale to the otherwise
impersonal scene by comparing it to 'a tent which had the whole
heath for its floor'.

This is the next paragraph:

> *The heaven being spread with this pallid screen and the
> earth with the darkest vegetation, their meeting-line at the
> horizon was clearly marked. In such contrast the heath
> wore the appearance of an instalment of night which
> had taken up its place before its astronomical hour was
> come: darkness had to a great extent arrived hereon, while
> the day stood distinct in the sky. Looking upwards, a*

*furze-cutter would have been inclined to continue work;
looking down, he would have decided to finish his faggot
and go home. The distant rims of the world and of the
firmament seemed to be a division in time no less than
a division in matter. The face of the heath by its mere
complexion added half an hour to evening; it could in
like manner retard the dawn, sadden noon, anticipate
the frowning of storms scarcely generated, and intensify
the opacity of a moonless midnight to a cause of
shaking and dread.*

The first two sentences above are descriptive narrative devoid
of human reference: 'pallid screen' and 'darkest vegetation' are
largely generalizations without colour or form. The paragraph
continues with even more abstract language: 'an instalment of night',
'astronomical hour', and 'day stood distinct in the sky'. But then a
hypothetical person appears, 'a furze-cutter', who brings life to the
otherwise unmoving scene. If he looks up, he'll continue cutting
the fodder; if he looks down into the dark, he'll finish his bundle
and go home. Hardy not only creates life and movement with this
'character', he creates a sense of scale – the lone human figure in the
midst of this vast open space.

The sentence that ends the paragraph doesn't refer to a particular
person, but it does express a range of human emotions in describing
the effects of this strange darkening: the 'face' of the heath has
this 'complexion'; it can '*sadden* noon', 'anticipate the *frowning*
of storms', and turn 'moonless midnight to a cause of *shaking and
dread*' (my emphases). In this way, sadness, anger and fear are
evoked by the premature dark of the landscape, and the reader
relates the landscape to human emotion.

Writing can therefore be said to have 'character' without having any
characters, but by making a variety of references to human physical,
psychological and emotional traits.

Finding sources of character

The most basic source of writers' characters is the actual writer.
This doesn't mean that writers, especially experienced writers, are
essentially just writing about themselves. But most people tend to
project themselves into imagining other people. Their ideas about
others also involve ideas about themselves. This is also true of writers.

Key idea

The writer's life is the ultimate source of fictional characters.

In addition to themselves, writers also model characters and aspects of characters on their immediate families. Parents and siblings and spouses and partners and children serve in whole or part as models for characters and for relationships between characters. Writers use immediate and extended family memories to model characters of and at different ages. Friends and acquaintances can also be used in these ways. This means that the fictional character can be built from a number of 'real' traits in different people observed and recalled by the writer. This composite character becomes a whole character – someone else – in the creation of the work of fiction.

ASPECTS OF CHARACTER: *HUMBOLDT'S GIFT*

Many readers of Saul Bellow's 1975 novel **Humboldt's Gift** know that the title character, Von Humboldt Fleisher, is closely modelled on Bellow's friend and one-time mentor Delmore Schwartz, talented poet and prose writer, New York intellectual par excellence, and alcoholic manic-depressive.

Bellow even names the character as an exaggerated, comic rendition of Delmore Schwartz, with his unusual first name and common, often Jewish, surname Schwartz meaning 'black'. The 'Del' morphs into the German 'von' and the 'more' into 'Humboldt', so that his first name suggests great intellect and achievement – the von Humboldt brothers Wilhelm and Alexander being between them philosopher, diplomat, linguist, educational theorist, scientific geographer and explorer. The surname 'Fleisher' is a variant spelling of the German or Yiddish for 'butcher', suggesting the cruder part of Fleisher/Schwartz's nature as paranoid alcoholic manic-depressive.

Nor does Bellow limit the modelling to the name and mental and psychological traits. He describes Humboldt physically as '…with his wide-set gray eyes. He was fine as well as thick, heavy but also light.' 'Later he got a prominent belly, like Babe Ruth. His legs were restless and his feet made nervous movements. Below, shuffling comedy; above, princeliness and dignity, a certain nutty charm.' These could be descriptions of Delmore Schwartz.

What's more, the narrator and central character of the novel, Charlie Citrine, is a barely disguised version of Saul Bellow. Citrine is a famous prize-winning, wealthy writer. Films have been made of his books. He's divorced and has girlfriends and an ambivalent attitude to both Humboldt and to himself. At one point, Citrine thinks of himself as 'a higher-thought clown'. Much of the novel's plot and tension comes from Humboldt putting Charlie down for selling out while involving Charlie in plans and plots as Humboldt's own life spins ever faster out of control.

Just as Humboldt's name represents his split character, 'Charlie Citrine' suggests something less than he might appear. A citrine is only a semi-precious stone, and the colour citrine is lemon yellow. And 'Charlie isn't only short for 'Charles'; it also means 'a charlie', someone who's a credulous fool.

Bellow has more fun with names. He calls a wannabe hoodlum Rinaldo Cantabile. Cantabile is a wonderfully idiotic character, forever filled with screaming, apoplectic rage for not being taken seriously: 'cantabile' is the musical term for 'easy and flowing'.

Bellow doesn't always use names with such literal or ironic undertones, but they fit this high-spirited, flamboyant novel. *Humboldt's Gift* has an almost Dickensian zest to its characterization, and Dickens, of course, was the master of suggestive names, whether light-hearted and ironic or bitterly descriptive, such as the name of David Copperfield's cold, cruel and hard stepfather, Mr Murdstone.

Of course, characters' names don't have to indicate characters' traits, but writers have to name their characters and they have to feel comfortable with these names, that these names are right, that they somehow fit the conception of these characters. To this extent, naming characters is often closely related to the earliest stages of thinking about and creating characters – in other words, to the source of characters in the writing process.

There certainly is fiction, especially shorter fiction, in which a central character is unnamed – this is often the first-person narrator (as in Pushkin's short story 'The Shot'). You can never or almost never say 'never' about fiction, but for the most part writers work better naming characters at the start of the writing process, even though they may change a name later on.

Sometimes, writers, and I'm one of them, take care to name a central character something unlike their own names if the material is very autobiographical as a way of creating the relative objectivity needed to shape character and plot most effectively.

Key idea

Naming characters can be part of creating characters.

Returning to *Humboldt's Gift*, Bellow's sources for the two main male characters were in a way available as general knowledge to his literate readers, but chance put me in the way of understanding another of Bellow's sources, this time not for a whole character but for aspects of a character.

A few years before the publication of *Humboldt's Gift*, I was visiting New York, staying at a friend's apartment. At the time, my friend was seeing a woman I'll call Clara (not her real name). My friend told me that Clara had been a girlfriend of Saul Bellow. When she and I met, we asked the usual questions – where were we from? what did we do? She told me she was born and raised in a strict Pennsylvania Dutch Amish community, adding that she was no longer a believer. I could see that. This was at the height of the miniskirt era, and she wore hers very high. As well as her background, what was memorable were Clara's knees. She was genuinely knock-kneed, and pretty with it.

When I read the novel, I came across the character Anna Dempster Vonghel, called Demmie, a girlfriend of Citrine. Bellow wrote: '"There's a Dutch corner in Delaware," said Demmie. "And that's where the Vonghels came from."' She goes on to describe her young life of delinquency, and then adds, '"But I also know about three thousand Bible verses. Brought up on hellfire and damnation."' At this point I wondered if this might have been taken from Clara's background.

Then, after describing Demmie's eyes and face – which didn't particularly strike me as very like Clara's – Citrine says, 'But I fell first for her legs. They were extraordinary. And these beautiful legs had an exciting defect – her knees touched and her feet were turned outward so that when she walked fast the taut silk of her stockings made a slight sound of friction.'

Pennsylvania might have shifted into Delaware, but that was Clara's background and those were Clara's knees. What I saw then was how a writer can *compose* a character, making what's literally a composite into what in the writing becomes a unified person. The knees and the strict Dutch background now belong to Demmie. The writer's use of such selected details helps give the character living particularity.

Create a character

Take a minor character from one of your pieces of fiction and, without considering the original context, change her/him by adding two new, specific details. One should be physical – face or body – and the other should be a detail of the character's background. One of these details should be your own; the other should be from someone you know. Then, in first-person narration, introduce the character and these details in the opening of a piece of fiction of about 750 words (about two or three pages). The idea is to begin to create a character who interests you.

Now imagine a novel whose two main characters are both male writers. They're old friends. But one of them is rich and famous from his writing and the other is a critical and financial failure. The failure, jealous of his friend's success, thinks of ways to foil and humiliate him and these ways provide the novel's plot. But we've just done that novel in the case study of *Humboldt's Gift,* right? No, this is another, later novel. This is the outline story of Martin Amis's novel *The Information*, published in 1995.

Key idea

Characters can come from what you know professionally, from what you've read (or watched or heard) or from a setting you want to write about.

ASPECTS OF CHARACTER: *THE INFORMATION*

The Information is a good example of all three of these source areas. Both main characters are writers, and as someone who has spent his professional life as a writer, Amis is obviously knowledgeable about all sorts of details of the profession. He knows not only the act of writing but all the business of placing the writing through an agent, of dealing with editors and editors' assistants, and publicity departments, and sales strategies, and going on tours and giving readings and signings, and going to festivals, and doing research and jotting down ideas, and feeling pleased or unhappy with what he writes on any day.

The Information also comes from reading and admiring Bellow's writing, especially *Humboldt's Gift*. Though I'm exaggerating,

Amis's novel could be thought of as *Humboldt's Gift* told from Humboldt's point of view.

The Information is filled with characters who, to various extents, arise out of the same West London setting Amis has used before. This is, or was, an area where seedy streets can be only a few blocks away from elegant streets, and where low life and high life can be observed by middle-class writers or writers of no known class at all. All sorts of shoulders can be rubbed or shoved or fondled here.

Unlike *Humboldt's Gift,* in which both Humboldt and Citrine are good writers, the two novelists in *The Information* are truly terrible writers, but terrible writers of two different kinds. Richard Tull is so aware of every nuance of literary possiblity that his writing is complex and impacted to the point of being unreadable. Richard's literary career is summarized by the narrator:

> *... Richard Tull published his first novel,* Aforethought, *in Britain and America. If you homogenized all the reviews... allowing for many grades of generosity and IQ, then the verdict on* Aforethought *was as follows: nobody understood it, or even finished it, but, equally, nobody was sure it was shit. Richard flourished. ... Three years later, by which time he had become Books and Arts Editor of a little magazine called* The Little Magazine *(little then, and littler now), Richard published his second novel,* Dreams Don't Mean Anything *[an allusion to Delmore Schwartz's famous story 'In Dreams Begin Responsibilities'] in Britain but not in America. His third novel wasn't published anywhere. Neither was his fourth. Neither was his fifth. ... He had plenty of offers for his sixth because, by that time, during a period of cretinous urges and lurches, he had started responding to the kind of advertisements that plainly came out with it and said, WE WILL PUBLISH YOUR BOOK and AUTHORS WANTED (or was it NEEDED?) BY LONDON PUBLISHER. Of course, these publishers, crying out for words on paper like pining dogs under a plangent moon, weren't regular publishers. You paid them, for example. And, perhaps more importantly, no one ever read you.*

Richard's old friend and college roommate, Gwyn Barry, is a very different kind of very bad writer. Here is the narrator, describing Gwyn's kind of very bad from Richard's point of view:

[of Gwyn's first novel, Summertown] *The Gwyn figure,*
who narrated, was wan and Welsh, the sort of character
who, according to novelistic convention, quietly does all
the noticing – whereas reality usually sees to it that the
perspiring mute is just a perspiring mute, with nothing to
contribute. Still, the Gwyn figure, Richard conceded, was
the book's only strength: an authentic dud, a dud insider,
who brought back hard news from the dud world. ... It
tried to be 'touching'; but the only touching thing about
Summertown *was that it* thought *it was a novel. On*
publication it met with modest sales and (Richard again)
disgracefully unmalicious reviews.

This second book is the one that becomes super famous and
makes Gwyn super famous and super rich. By this time, Richard
has suffered 12 years of failure and he 'had to see whether the
experience of disappointment was going to make him bitter or
better. And it made him bitter. He was sorry: there was nothing he
could do about it, he wasn't up to better.'

As these extracts indicate, *The Information* is social satire as well
as a particular satire on the literary life. What links these two
satires is what can be thought of as a third level of satire – that on
male aggression and competitiveness – between writers, between
criminals, between races and classes.

To name or not to name?

Write a 150–250-word opening to a piece of fiction in the third
person, past tense, in which you introduce a character without
naming her/him or even particularly thinking of a name. Then write
this opening again, naming this character in your first sentence. Does
naming the character make a difference to the writing that follows?

Settings as sources of character

Settings as sources of character become particularly significant when
the setting is historical. One way of understanding what's involved
is to think of the fiction that actually comes from the past. Jane
Austen's settings, for instance, determine her heroines' chances of
happiness and success within the particular early nineteenth-century

English, semi-rural middle- and upper-middle-class families that can provide wives for local grandees – the squires and minor aristocrats who will settle down in marriage on their comfortable estates.

The heroines' chances for such happy endings occur within a convention of visits, teas, dinners and dances, with the occasional unplanned encounter while walking or riding in town or country to enliven and complicate plot. Even when money is short and the heroines' villa, grange or large farmhouse must be left for a fairly, but not very, humble cottage, these young women's good sense and good taste will lend the dwelling enough charm so that the convention of visiting will continue to bring them into contact with potential life partners.

While the Austen heroine is typically part of these social conventions by birth and upbringing ('breeding'), she can also see through their superficiality. Her intelligence and sensitivity can make her uncomfortably out of place, and her hatred of unkindness can lead her to the wrong conclusions about people, men in particular, the path out from confusion becoming the plotline of the novel.

This influence of particular social setting as a character 'source' is really another way of thinking about the character as influenced and developed, but not entirely determined, by the time and place of the setting.

An even more stringent historical determinant is fiction centred on real people. Hilary Mantel's novels about Thomas Cromwell are clear examples. The problem is obvious: how does the writer stick with the historical reality and yet create a character? First, she must not contradict the known facts of the character, including his physical appearance, while creating his thoughts, reflections, hopes, dreams – his inner life, a life which is not known – and while creating his particular actions and reactions, dialogue and his accompanying emotions – his outer life. Second, such facts and acts of his life that are known and that she chooses to include must be accurate enough to the historical record to appear plausible and, even if given a non-standard emphasis, must be read as representing a version of the historical record. Finally, she must make the character interesting, and even if he is monstrous – and Cromwell was – his courage and craft, his sense of humour and genuine love of scholarship, his hard work, his generosity and his warmth within his family must also hold the stage to develop this most complex yes-man and hatchet man.

The writer doesn't have to go back to Tudor or Regency England for historical sources of character. Even a book so seemingly timeless as Cormac McCarthy's *All the Pretty Horses*, a rite-of-passage or coming-of-age novel, is very time-specific. Set in 1949, John Grady Cole is the 16-year-old, last-of-the-line descendant of Texas ranchers whose values are alien to the changing America around him. So he rides out over the border, in search of the simpler, more natural land and lifestyle he imagines in Mexico. But the Mexico he finds also has telephones and cars and trucks and wealthy landowners who won't have a *Yanqui* nobody courting their beloved daughter. The historical setting turns out to mark a final disappearance of the dream of open land and life yearned for by the boy-man. Set half a generation later, the story would be impossible. It is, as much as anything, a novel of disappearances.

People as sources of character

The variety of sources for character is as varied as the lives – the experiences, the memories and the imaginations – of writers. Here are some sources of fictional characters in my own writing:

- me
- my father
- my mother
- my uncle
- a woman who lived in a house in the dunes by the ocean in Long Island
- a very well-dressed man I once saw walking in a rough neighbourhood of Brooklyn
- someone I knew in high school who became very arrogant
- a publisher I knew who was very arrogant
- someone I heard about who was rumoured to have an ancestor who found Captain Kidd's treasure
- a Navaho man I spoke with outside a store in the Four Corners area of Arizona
- Hamlet
- Sam Spade
- Raskolnikov and Svidrigailov
- Kurosawa's film of *The Idiot*
- some irritatingly over-friendly waiting staff at a popular outdoor restaurant in Key West.

All the fictional characters derived from these sources had traits from other people and from my imagination.

Key idea

A partial or major source for an aspect of one character in a work of fiction can be another character in that work. Aspects of character are changed and developed in the writing (and rewriting) of the work; sometimes the work demands the omission of a character and/or the inclusion of a new character.

Workshop

Select a piece of writing from your portfolio that has two characters that you consider well achieved and interesting. The piece can be anything from a very short story to the draft of a complete novel. Then answer the following questions about the source or sources of these characters.

- Were any of their traits consciously drawn from your own traits?
- If not consciously drawn, do you now see any of your own traits in these characters?
- Were any of their traits drawn from family, friends or acquaintances?
- If so, were either of these characters substantially modelled on a family member, friend or acquaintance?
- Was any real character a significant source for either of these characters?
- Was any fictional character a partial source for these characters?
- If not, do you think you might ever be able to use a book or books you admire to give you an idea for a character?

Choosing either of these characters, what particular combination of traits do you think makes her/him interesting to write about and to read about?

Finally, after considering these questions, do you think you followed your sources too closely, not closely enough or just about right?

Focus points

- When writing is said to have 'character' without having any characters, it often means it's lively and distinctive through a variety of references to human physical, psychological and emotional traits.
- The most basic source of writers' characters is the actual writer. Writers also model characters and aspects of characters on their family and friends.
- Characters can also come from what we know professionally and socially, and from real events and settings.

Next step

The next chapter moves from sources of character to an initial consideration of general character types.

2

General character types: flat

Characters in fiction can be thought of as comprising two very general types, flat and round. These designations were first put forward by E.M. Forster in *Aspects of the Novel* (1927). Flat characters can be thought of as undeveloped, or sketched, or comprising one or just a few characteristics. Round, or rounded, characters are those developed in depth.

It's important to note that this doesn't mean that flat characters are in themselves either bad or good, just as round characters aren't as such either good or bad. It's also most useful to think of flat and round characters being on two ends of a continuum of development, so that there can be very flat and less flat characters, and there can be highly developed and less developed round characters.

Characters in fiction

What is the character of characters? Another way to put the question is: what distinguishes characters in fiction from characters in other art forms?

On the face of it, theatre seems the most direct and powerful way to experience characters in art. After all, there they are, living people speaking and in action right in front of us. We see exactly what they look like, we hear exactly what they say and how they say it, and, if the acting is good, we don't think of the actor playing a role, we watch Blanche or Hedda or Ophelia struggling to survive with some dignity. What's more, we can watch their actions at the same time that we hear them speak. That isn't literally possible on the page we read. And in cinema and television we can see the emotions changing on the characters' faces – in close-up – as they argue; Blanche may still be protesting, but Stanley's insinuations have her close to tears. Fiction has no such simultaneity. Or we're watching the film, driving along with Thelma and Louise as they're about to escape, and then we're hanging 3,000 feet over the Grand Canyon with the two of them, dizzy with the drop. What words on the page can bring on such sudden vertigo?

Nevertheless, I'm not arguing myself out of a job because, though everything above is true, fiction can offer its readers an experience of characters deeper and more intense and immediate than other arts. The reason is that the characters in fiction are created not only by the writers but also by the readers as they read.

Key idea

Guided by the writing, readers of fiction create their own particular image of a character. They see and hear the character in a way stated by the words on the page, but the character is also shaped by their own *responding imaginations*. It's this responding imagination, the readers' creativity, that can make the characters more real to readers than characters in plays and cinema. Those characters look exactly as they look, sound exactly as they sound. But the characters read in good fiction look, sound and act like something partly created by the readers. This is the uniqueness of fiction, its ultimate power.

Flat characters and plot

The characters in many folk and fairy tales represent the extreme of flat characters. They react rather than think. Some characters are morally good, some bad, and others are neither good nor bad, but they remain unchanged throughout the tale. The action in these tales is paramount. The characters have no time to reflect; they just act.

Here are some examples of the openings of Russian fairy tales:

> *One upon a time there was an old man who lived with his old wife. The husband planted a head of cabbage in the cellar and the wife planted one in the ash bin.*

The characters are named only 'old man' and 'old wife'. No reason is given for the odd behaviour that starts the story, but this is enough to want to know what happens next.

> *A hen and a cock were walking in the priest's barnyard. Suddenly the cock began to choke on a bean. The hen was sorry for him, so she went to the river to ask for some water. The river answered: 'Go to the lime tree and ask for a leaf; then I will give you some water.'*

Here the characters are animals, a river and a lime tree. But they act as human characters. Anything can be a character, even inanimate objects, and they're all of the same undeveloped nature.

> *In a certain village there lived two peasants, blood brothers; one was poor and the other rich.*

In this tale, all that differentiates the brothers is their wealth. And 'In a certain village' gives the same information as 'once upon a time'; that is, no specific information at all, except the important signal that this is a tale.

> *Grandfather planted a turnip. The time came to pick it. He took hold of it and pulled and pulled, but he couldn't pull it out. Grandfather called grandmother; grandmother pulled grandfather, and grandfather pulled the turnip. They pulled and pulled, but they couldn't pull it out.*

These could be the same old man and his old wife who planted cabbages in the first example. What might happen next? And after that?

> *The king of a certain country lost his ring while on a drive through its capital. He at once placed a notice in the newspapers, promising that whoever might find his ring would receive a large reward in money. A simple private was lucky enough to find it.*

The king wants something – his ring. The lowly private wants something – his reward. These absolutely flat characters have all it takes to get a story going.

> *In a certain city there lived a merchant who had three sons: the first was Fyodor, the second Vasily, and the third Ivan the fool.*

At last some characters are named. But this is only to differentiate the first two from Ivan the fool. Ivan not only has a name, he has a trait: he's a fool. But readers of or listeners to tales are usually wary of believing that a 'fool' will act foolishly, especially in Russian tales.

What these tales have in common, besides their paper-thin characters, is their super-fast plots. Something happens in the first or second sentence that causes something else to happen in the second or third. And so it goes on until the last sentence. The action takes precedence over character development or detailed description. What we can make of character depends on what each character does and on cultural expectation.

These are the most obvious flat characters. They are barely 'types', they have such meagre attributes. What is less obvious is that fiction which can strike us as much deeper and much more developed can also be created from relatively flat characters.

THE USES OF FLAT CHARACTERS

Here is the opening paragraph of Flannery O'Connor's short story 'The Comforts of Home', published in 1965.

> *Thomas withdrew to the side of the windows and with his head between the wall and the curtain he looked down on the driveway where the car had stopped. His mother and the little slut were getting out of it. His mother emerged slowly,*

*stolid and awkward, and then the little slut's long slightly
bowed legs slid out, the dress pulled above the knees. With
a shriek of laughter she ran to meet the dog, who bounded,
overjoyed, shaking with pleasure, to welcome her. Rage
gathered throughout Thomas's large frame with a silent
ominous intensity, like a mob assembling.*

The third-person narration in the first sentence is omniscient, at
a distance from Thomas. But it shifts in the second sentence with
the violent conjunction of 'His mother and the little slut' into a
limited omniscience from Thomas's point of view. In fact, 'mother'
and 'little slut' will be the two flat characters who provide the
plot's dynamics, 'mother' representing the original stability Thomas
struggles to maintain against the destabilizing, disorienting power
of 'the little slut'.

Once Thomas's point of view is established, we tend to read the
description of the two women as his own. When we read that his
mother 'emerged slowly, stolid and awkward', we see it as a fair
physical and emotional description of Thomas himself, before the
'little slut' appeared. As for the other woman ('the other woman'
in its adulterous sense as well): 'the little slut's long slightly bowed
legs slid out, the dress pulled above the knees.' While Thomas's view
of his mother is a generalization, a taken-for-granted glance at a
known shape, 'stolid' suggesting furniture-like familiarity, his view
of the other woman lingers voyeuristically in its detail: 'and then the
little slut's long slightly bowed legs slid out, the dress pulled above
the knees.' The legs didn't appear, they 'slid', and the adjectives
preceding 'legs' imitate the long, sinuous slide of Thomas's peeping
(who 'withdrew to the side of the window … with his head between
the wall and the curtain') in its repressed sexuality.

The next sentence – 'With a shriek of laughter she ran to meet
the dog, who bounded, overjoyed, shaking with pleasure, to
welcome her' – seems to alter the point of view. The 'shriek' is how
Thomas would hear her, a sound appropriate for 'the little slut'.
But the dog's response can only be the more objective narrator's
voice, since 'overjoyed', 'pleasure' and 'welcome' are exactly what
Thomas is incapable of feeling – consciously, that is. The most
striking phrase here is 'shaking with pleasure', with its totally
uninhibited, near orgastic connotations. The following sentence
ends the paragraph: 'Rage gathered throughout Thomas's large
frame with a silent ominous intensity, like a mob assembling.' This,
completely Thomas's point of view, is his conscious reaction to his
subconscious, repressed sexual excitement.

And the following one-sentence paragraph is his visceral response – flight: 'It was now up to him to pack a suitcase, go to the hotel, and stay there until the house should be cleared.' He cannot even think of the girl here as a human. That the house should be 'cleared' reduces her to some sort of infestation or communicable disease.

The next paragraph begins with his list of negatives: 'did not know', disliked', 'was not portable', 'could not bear', which, with the books 'he needed' and the electric blanket 'he was used to' (as opposed to the warmth of another human body) are the inertial forces, the comforts of home, that check his flight.

Thomas's conclusion, that his mother 'was about to wreck the peace of the house', turns his flight into fight, his homely declaration of war.

Key idea

A character might have a complex without being a complex character. The character, that is, may still be relatively flat.

Create a flat character

In about 300 words, introduce a potentially flat character, using third-person narration, as observed by another character. Make the reader understand something significant about the relation between the observer and the observed.

In 'The Comforts of Home', the story's opening paragraphs occur towards the midpoint of the story's chronology. Thomas's mother feels duty-bound to save this wayward girl and has brought her home for supper, against Thomas's wishes. Thomas has checked up on the girl, Star, and found out that she is a 'psychotic personality, not insane enough for the asylum, not criminal enough for the jail, not stable enough for society'. Now, a few pages on, all three characters are together.

'Thomas writes history,' his mother said with a threatening look at him. 'He's president of the local Historical Society this year.'

The girl leaned forward and gave Thomas an even more pointed attention. 'Fabulous!' she said in a throaty voice.

'Right now Thomas is writing about the first settlers in this county,' his mother said.

'Fabulous!' the girl repeated.

Thomas by an effort of will managed to look as if he were alone in the room.

'Say, you know who you look like?' Star asked, her head on one side, taking him in at an angle.

'Oh, some one very distinguished!' his mother said archly.

'This cop I saw in the movie I went to last night,' Star said.

'Star,' his mother said, 'I think you ought to be careful about the kind of movies you go to. I think you ought to see only the best ones. I don't think crime stories would be good for you.'

'Oh this was a crime-does-not-pay,' Star said, 'and I swear this cop looked exactly like him. They were always putting something over on the guy. He would look like he couldn't stand it a minute longer or he would blow up. He was a riot. And not bad looking,' she added with an appreciative leer at Thomas.

Even in the story's opening scene, Star seems more than a simple 'type', more than 'the tramp' or the 'dumb slut'. She understands how to deal with Thomas's mother by giving a moralistic response to the moralistic admonition about dangerous movies. And though, true to type, she flirts with Thomas, she's sensitive enough to pick up his embarrassment and clever enough to tease him by comparing his discomfort to that of the cop in the film. Of course, there's just so far this cleverness extends. For instance, when, speaking of the cop (and, by extension, Thomas), she says, 'He was a riot,' she means it only in the sense of being very funny. It's the narrator/writer who also suggests the darker meaning of 'riot' linking this back to 'Rage gathered throughout Thomas's large frame with a silent ominous intensity, *like a mob assembling*' [my emphasis]. You could say that, although Star is true to type, there's more to her than merely type.

Another way to state this is that a perfectly flat character can't really surprise the reader but a slightly rounded flat character, like Star, can.

As for Thomas's mother, she certainly is a two-dimensional character. Completely predictable, completely unchangeable, the author never even names her in the story. She makes the story go, of course, but that is her function. She has a characteristic of moralistic, conventional charity, a characteristic of complete belief in her values as making her a good person from a good family, and – important for the plot mechanisms it offers – a naive, easily gullible faith in her power to change someone unlucky enough not to be conventionally good.

Her type is the superficial good mother, in which custom and convention substitute for any real moral or psychological intelligence.

And Thomas? I've suggested that he has a complex without being a complex character. I don't think it's what Freudians would call an Oedipus complex because there's nothing in the story that indicates that he has any conscious or unconscious sexual desire/ fantasy concerning his mother. At the same time, he is 'wed' to the comforts of the home his mother has run before Star turns up. So he can be thought of as settled into the kind of sexless existence that some older couples can have. At the same time, there's nothing in the story to indicate that he may be unconsciously gay. There is, however, plenty to indicate that he isn't asexual: O'Connor's descriptive language of his rage and anger is typically, allusively and metaphorically, sexual.

Perhaps Thomas's emotional struggle is to maintain his asexual status against the disturbing implications of his sexuality as awakened in the rage caused by the girl's flagrant advances.

He is nevertheless a flat character, though rounded by this 'complex' and by his intellect and scholarship, which he applies to researching Star's background and in argument about her with his mother. He conforms to the type of the 'unworldly academic' defending the ivory tower of his home. And he fights to the end, and a bitter end it is, against changing.

If you know Flannery O'Connor's fiction, and you should, you find that many of her characters are flat in that they live by an inflexible and narrow set of standards – social or religious – and are often victims of their inflexibility at the hands of amoral flat characters who will have their violent way, even if, as in this story, they force the 'better' characters into their own reactive violence, or, as the author put it in the title of her novella, *The Violent Bear It Away*. Flanner O'Connor's fiction at its best exemplifies that writing can be profound about various degrees of flat character when it's so word perfect.

Write a scene with flat characters

Write a 750-word scene involving two or three relatively flat but not necessarily simple characters. Write in the third person, in the past or present tense, with an omniscient or limited omniscient point of view or a combination of the two. This could be a development from the last Snapshot exercise or a reworking of a scene from your fiction portfolio. You can, if you wish, model your characters on O'Connor's 'Southern Gothic' or 'Southern Grotesque', substituting a regionalism with which you feel comfortable.

It's only fair to say that my thinking on flat characters differs from E.M. Forster's in that he held that truly tragic characters could not be at all flat. On the other hand, Flannery O'Conner's fiction wasn't around in 1927 when he wrote about this. But I certainly agree with his views on the usefulness of flat characters in the novel.

> *One great advantage of flat characters is that they are easily recognized whenever they come in – recognized by the reader's emotional eye, not by the visual eye, which merely notes the recurrence of a proper name. … It is a convenience for an author when he can strike with his full force at once, and flat characters are very useful to him, since they never need reintroducing, never run away, have not to be watched for development, and provide their own atmosphere – little luminous discs of a pre-arranged size, pushed hither and thither like counters across the void or between the stars; most satisfactory.*

> *A second advantage is that they are easily remembered by the reader afterwards. They remain in his mind as unalterable for the reason that they were not changed by circumstances; they moved through circumstances, which gives them in retrospect a comforting quality, and preserves them when the book that produced them may decay.*
> E.M. Forster, *Aspects of the Novel*

TYPES OF FLAT CHARACTER

At this point, it's worth distinguishing between some terms often applied to flat characters.

The term 'stereotype', coming from metals cast as letters that keep their shape, means as applied to fiction a character who does not change. And 'stereotype' is also applied to a fictional character whom readers find merely boring or morally offensive because of a set of negative physical, mental, and/or social characteristics of race, class, gender, sexuality, nationality, religious belief, age and so on. A stereotyped character may also be flat without being negatively presented in a generally morally offensive way, as above. Whether a stereotyped – that is, unchanging – character is boring is naturally a case-by-case consideration.

The term 'type' is more flexibly applied to fictional characters. This is very similar to the colloquial use, as in 'She's the type who's always there when you need her,' or 'He's the strong, silent type.' Flat literary characters may be thought of as any number of types, such as 'the bristling military man', 'the love-struck teenage girl', 'the talkative taxi driver', 'the whining child', 'the quiet librarian', 'the jolly friar', 'the noisy drinker', and on and on.

The more that types are differentiated, the less flat they become:

1 The student
2 The poor student
3 The poor student nihilist
4 The poor student nihilist who murders a pawnbroker
5 The poor student nihilist who murders a pawnbroker and yet is inherently good.

By the time we get to the fourth example you have Raskolnikov. By the fifth, you have a short statement of the plot and theme of *Crime and Punishment*.

But it's of little use to typify the three main characters of 'The Comforts of Home' as 'the do-gooder mother', 'the slut' and the 'repressed mama's boy intellectual', since in the story their behaviour 'to type' is only one of the several ways they behave. They are, to various degrees, what Forster calls 'rounded flat characters'.

Short stories provide a wide diversity of flat characters partly *because* they're short. There isn't the space to develop fully more than one or two characters.

MIXING ROUND AND FLAT CHARACTERS

In James Joyce's short story '**Clay**' (1914), for example, there are two developed characters, the main character Maria and her younger brother Joe, a 'rounded' flat character. Maria is single, what would have been called a 'spinster' when the story was written. She works and lives at a large Dublin laundry. Here's her initial description:

> *Maria was a very, very small person indeed, but she had a very long nose and a very long chin. She talked a little through her nose, always soothingly: 'Yes, my dear,' and 'No, my dear.' She was always sent for when the women quarrelled over their tubs and always succeeded in making peace. One day the Matron had said to her:*
>
> *'Maria, you are a veritable peace-maker!'*
>
> *And the sub-matron and two of the Board ladies had heard the compliment. And Ginger Mooney was always saying what she wouldn't do to the dummy who had charge of the irons if it wasn't for Maria. Everyone was so fond of Maria.*

The story follows Maria as she leaves work and makes her way to Joe's home on All Hallows' Eve, buying presents of cakes for her brother and sister-in-law and nieces and nephews and the neighbour children who will be there. When Maria takes time to decide on a special cake to bring the adults, the young woman serving her, annoyed, asks whether she wants wedding cake. Maria blushes but thinks only that the young woman was a little annoyed at the time she was taking. There are interactions with other people as she makes her way to her brother's house, each showing her genuine kindness and innocence. Through it all, Joyce never lets the reader forget how small and odd-looking Maria is, as in 'She got out of her tram at the Pillar and ferreted her way quickly among the crowds.' Ferreted: the quick motion of a small creature with a pointed nose.

During her journey, her thoughts turn to Joe, so by the time she arrives at the house we know a lot about him: he is kind, but not when he's drunk: 'He was so different when he took any drink.' He and his wife had offered that she live with them, but Maria was happier with her independence in her own little room at the laundry. And Joe was looked after as a child by Maria. He often said, 'Mamma is mamma, but Maria is my proper mother.'

At Joe's, Maria finds that she's left the special cake she bought on the tram, distracted as she was by the friendly civility of a man who was extremely polite to her, sign of a real gentleman, she thought, 'even when he has a drop taken'. Joe is very nice with her until Maria thinks to put in a good word for their brother Alphy, from whom Joe is estranged. At this, Joe nearly loses his temper, but his wife reminds him that this is a night for the children to enjoy, and Joe relents. During the festivities, the next-door girls puts saucers out holding different objects and lead the children up to it blindfolded. Whatever they touch will tell their future. So one touches a prayer book, predicting a life in religion, and others touch water, predicting travel, and one girl touches the saucer with a ring on it and is teased about a romance. Then they all insist Maria play, and as they blindfold her she laughs, 'and laughed again till the tip of her nose nearly touched the tip of her chin'. Then she puts her hand out and it comes down on a 'soft wet substance', and everyone falls silent until someone mentions 'the garden' and Joe's wife crossly tells one of the next-door girls to throw it out at once. Maria realizes only that she's played the game incorrectly and she does it over again and gets the prayer book.

Then the party becomes cheery again and Maria has never seen Joe so nice to her as he was then, and when the children become sleepy Joe asks Maria to sing for them before she goes. Accompanied by her sister-in-law on the piano, Maria sings two verses of 'I Dreamt that I Dwelt' but instead of singing the second verse she repeats the first. Nobody mentions this.

> *... and when she had ended her song Joe was very much moved. He said that there was no time like the long ago and no music for him like poor old Balfe, whatever other people might say; and his eyes filled up so much with tears that he could not find what he was looking for and in the end he had to ask his wife to tell him where the corkscrew was.*

And this ends the story.

I've spent some time with this summary in order to explain the importance of the minor, flattish character Joe in relation to the main, well-developed character Maria, and this isn't about their brother–sister relationship but about their functional relationship in creating the story's emotional depth and narrative continuity.

The first half of the story introduces Maria and narrates the end of her day's work, her changing for the party, and her shopping for the children's and adults' presents. Joe appears here only in her thoughts and in reflective flashback. She is never referred to as 'midget' or 'dwarf', and as she undresses and stands before her mirror, Joyce writes, 'she looked with quaint affection at the diminutive body which she had so often adorned. In spite of its years she found it a nice tidy little body.' Whatever others may think of her tininess, she is comfortable with herself. Joyce describes her with a dignity that makes her naivety charming rather than pathetic. The scene above, before her mirror, surprises us and then shames us that we should be surprised she isn't a stereotyped self-loathing 'freak'. We follow her through her travels across the city and into shops to buy just the right things for her family, through the taunting of the irritated shop girl and on to a crowded tram where none of the young men notices her but an 'elderly gentleman' makes room for her. And nothing dampens her good spirits but the realization that she's left the special cake bought for the adults on the tram.

But Joe tells her it doesn't matter and is kind to her, so she's happy once again. And now, as well as us readers, there's Joe and his wife to observe her. It's his wife who becomes angry about the object from the garden, the clay of the story's title, on the saucer Maria first chooses. Maria understands only that something went wrong in the game and she must choose again, but Joe and his wife have seen the clay in her hand as the clay she must come to and can't allow Maria to see it, too.

What affects Joe even more is Maria's mistake with the song lyrics. The song, one of the most popular of the nineteenth century, has a first verse which begins, 'I dreamt that I dwelt in marble halls,' but Maria sings this twice, rather than the second verse's actual lyrics: 'I dreamt that suitors sought my hand.'

It's Joe who's moved by this mistake, Joe who has tears in his eyes for this and for the clay that Maria (and he) will become, and for her deformed face and small child-sized body and her loneliness and lack of husband and children, and maybe for her bravery and independence, though he may have little idea of her very real satisfactions.

Without this relatively flat character of Joe, the story couldn't reveal how he and we are affected, because Joyce's third-person narrator is not going to point out – to editorialize – the sentiment we should feel and by doing so turn it into sentimentality. And this is the functional relationship between Joe and Maria, to articulate and/or embody an emotional reality, and a stylistic coherence in which narration stays distinct from characters *showing* the reader characters through their actions and speech.

Key idea

By reaction and interaction, flatter characters can give more developed characters emotional and interpretive depth.

Novels, of course, may have a wider range of characters that can be thought of as flat to various degrees.

Imagine that one of your main, fully developed characters, Philip, takes a taxi to get somewhere. Here are some of the options open to you as the writer:

1 Philip caught a cab at 22nd Street and made it to the meeting just as it began.

2 Philip caught a taxi at Regent's Park and asked the driver whether he could make it to Marble Arch in ten minutes. The driver said he didn't think so.

3 Philip caught a cab at 22nd Street and asked the driver whether she could make it to the Metropolitan Museum of Art in twenty minutes. She said, 'Yeah, me and Superwoman,' and Philip's heart sank.

4 Philip caught a taxi at Regent's Park and asked the driver whether he could make it to Marble Arch in ten minutes. When he said he couldn't, Philip asked whether a ten-pound tip would make a difference. 'Right, gov'nor,' he said, putting his tabloid paper down and half turning his head back, 'I'd have your tenner and lose my licence.'

5 Philip caught a cab at 22nd Street and asked whether the driver, a man with long black hair and a yellow bandana around it, could get to the Metropolitan Museum of Art in twenty minutes. 'Sure, sure,' he said, 'no vorry.' He pulled out into the traffic and said, 'Vat place you say me?' Philip repeated, 'The Metropolitan Museum of Art.' 'Yes, sure, sure. Big museum, I know.' Philip sat back, relieved. Then the driver said, 'Vere is museum?'

The first option doesn't mention the driver. Only the hurry is important. The second option has a character so minimal, so flat, that he gets only an indirect quote. In the third, you decide to characterize the driver by some big-city sarcasm highlighting the impossibility of Philip's request and causing Philip's reaction. In the fourth option, you first give the cabbie indirect speech; and when this leads to Philip's asking whether money can change his mind, the driver gets direct speech – a bit more development – in explaining why the extra money wouldn't be worth it.

The fifth option creates a flat character that's the most memorable of this lot. But it costs you the most words. You give him physical description and dialogue and an accent and almost no knowledge of the city; you've written a complete little scene of dialogue for this driver. So you must be thinking that it's not only interesting (funny) in itself, but that it develops Philip's predicament at the right pace and that its tone fits with the overall tone of the novel.

Will you continue the scene? Will Philip look at the cab driver's displayed photo and see that it looks nothing like the driver? It depends, doesn't it? When you bring a character out of the background oblivion (options 1 and 2) into a bit of light (options 3 and 4), or turn up the illumination (option 5), there are usually a number of considerations determining your choice.

It should be understood that I'm referring to what you, the writer, finally end up with. Of course, as you first write, it may be longer or shorter or with a different emphasis than your final draft.

 ## Key idea

Flat characters can be useful for structural purposes.

Writing to his editor about the structure of *Under the Volcano*, Malcolm Lowry explained that he used the Faustus story (Marlowe's *Dr Faustus* as well as Goethe's *Faust*) as a template for his novel. He said that this was intended for his own use rather than as a structure he wanted his readers to be aware of. In other words, its chief purpose was to give him, as the writer, points of reference helpful in the novel's composition.

This loose 'template' idea was useful to me in writing the novel *Virgil's Ghost*. It's a modern detective story for which I used Dante's *Inferno* as a rough template for both plot and character. The main character figuratively goes through hell – New York City in this instance – from the beginning of the book until he leaves it at the very end to face his own secular purgatory. If a reader picked up the Dante references, fine, but I intended them primarily for my own use.

A number of flat characters arose from this. Early in the book, the first of these is Gerry Santini, a police pathologist my main character Lenny Schwartz has worked with before quitting the force to become a private detective. I used imagery from Dante's least punished sinners, the illicit lovers who forever fly around without being able to catch one another. Here is how Santini appears.

He leapt from the car, shaking his wristwatch. 'Eleven minutes! Eleven from Police Plaza, over the bridge and through downtown Brooklyn to Fabulous Flatbush Avenue Extension. Ta-da!'

'Gerry, you're supposed to analyse corpses, not create them,' Schwartz said, holding both arms out to the sallow, handsome man.

'Well, business is slow, but never Santini,' he said, hugging Schwartz at the curb. He stepped back, his hands on Schwartz's shoulders. 'Fantastic! You look less like a private eye than you did a cop, and you never looked like a cop.'

And a few minutes later, he is speaking about Schwartz's marital problems with his wife Karen:

'...I've sort of guessed what the last four or five years have been for you and ... Jesus,' he laughed, as Schwartz's head hung lower, 'why am I being so nice? I've been lusting after Karen for years. She's far too good for you. What she needs, you know, is a fellow Catholic, I mean, another lapsed Catholic fellow. We could elapse, elope, share an excommunication and eternity flitting around each other's tail... Hey, Len! This is supposed to cheer you. I love you. I can say that because I'm a macho Italian male. We get a special dispensation for telling guys we love them without having to be gay.'

Here, Santini is himself referring to Dante's imagery for guilty lovers, but my point was to make him work in the structure, as well as to make him a literate minor character, not developed further than this wise guy surface, but hopefully interesting at that.

A little further on in the novel, another character appears based on my *Inferno* scheme, a grossly overweight underworld informer, whose name, Pignatelli, is my version of Dante's glutton Ciacco, literally 'pig', in the third circle of hell. Again, this naming isn't important for readers to pick up: it worked for me in writing the character, and the flat fat character worked to move the story into a further and worse level of crime.

A classic character

Think of a piece of classic literature that's a favourite of yours and then introduce a flatter type of minor character based on a character from that work in 300–500 words. Narrate this in the first person. (The narrator should not be the minor character of this exercise.)

Key idea

Flat fictional characters may be, but don't have to be, minor characters; nor is the fact of their flatness any indication of their literary quality.

Workshop

Select a piece of fiction from your portfolio – short story, novel or section of a novel – that you feel needs better characterization. Then ask yourself the following questions, perhaps writing down short answers to each.

- Who are the main characters and who are the minor characters?
- Remembering that the range of characterizations that can be called 'flat' does not necessarily mean poorly written or stereotyped, are any of these characters flat?
- Is any flat character also a minor character?
- If so, take a close, critical look at this flat minor character. Should she/he be made more of an individual, with more specific characteristics?
- Is this a question of the character's dialogue?
- Is this a question of the character's attitude towards a major character?
- Should the character be more intelligent or less intelligent?
- Is this a question of a specific action or reaction to another character, major or minor?

After these considerations and short answers, do a rewrite of this flat character to improve him/her.

After doing this rewrite, do you think that it might modify what you do to improve another character, major or minor, in the piece of fiction?

Focus points

- Characters in fiction are created not only by the writer but also by readers as they read. This is the power of fiction.
- Flat characters react rather than think or reflect and they remain unchanged throughout the tale.
- In some stories with flat characters, the action takes precedence over character development or detailed description, but even stories with relatively flat characters can create successful fiction.
- Minor, flattish characters can be important in relation to a main, well-developed character or characters in terms of creating a story's emotional depth and narrative continuity.

Next step

The next chapter continues to look at general character types, this time focusing on rounded, or more fully developed, characters.

3

General character types: rounded

Fully developed, or rounded, characters in fiction are usually those through whom the story or novel chiefly takes place. As with the flat characters, this general definition is not a statement of the literary quality of such characters; you will know that it's all too easy to think of writing in which the most developed characters are unsatisfactory.

While there is no single or best way of developing characters in depth, the examples in this chapter – and throughout this book – are taken from fiction that shows how successful characterization can operate. When a novel or short story opens, it often establishes the conditions of fully developed characters, especially the condition of *change*. This chapter looks at openings in which fully developed characters are introduced and examines what it is that holds your attention and why you want to read on.

Rounded characters and change

One major source of change in a character is the change in another character with whom they're in some intimate emotional and/or working relation. A good example of this begins Alison Lurie's 2005 novel *Truth and Consequences*.

On a hot midsummer morning, after sixteen years of marriage, Jane Mackenzie saw her husband fifty feet away and did not recognize him.

She was in the garden picking lettuce when the sound of a car stopping on the road by the house made her look up. Someone was getting out of the taxi, paying the driver, and then starting slowly down the long driveway: an aging man with slumped shoulders, a sunken chest, and a protruding belly, leaning on a cane. The hazy sun was in her eyes and she couldn't see his face clearly, but there was something about him that made her feel uneasy and a little frightened. He reminded her of other unwelcome figures: a property tax inspector who had appeared at the door soon after they moved into the house; an FBI official who was investigating one of Alan's former students; and the scruffy-looking guy who one summer two years ago used to stand just down the road where the ramp to the highway began, waving at passing cars and asking for a lift downtown. If you agreed, before he got out he would lean over the seat and in a half-whiney, half-threatening way ask for the 'loan' of a couple of dollars.

Then Jane's vision cleared, and she saw that it was her husband Alan Mackenzie, who shouldn't be there. Less than an hour ago she had driven him to the University, where he had a lunch meeting at the College of Architecture, and where she had expected him to stay until she picked him up that afternoon. Since he'd hurt his back fifteen months ago, he hadn't been able to drive. Jane snatched up her basket of lettuce and began to walk uphill, then almost to run.

'What's happened, what's the matter?' she called out when she was within range.

'Nothing,' Alan muttered, not quite looking at her. His cane grated on the gravel as he came to a slow halt. 'I didn't feel well, so I came home.'

'Is it very bad?' Jane put her hand on the creased sleeve of his white shirt. Crazy as it was, she still couldn't quite believe that the person inside the shirt was her husband. Alan wasn't anything like this, he was healthy and strong and confident, barely over fifty. This man had Alan's broad forehead and narrow straight nose and thick pale-brown hair, but he looked at least ten years older and twenty pounds heavier, and his expression was one of pain and despair. 'You said at breakfast you were all right – anyhow, no worse than usual...' Her voice trailed off.

'If you want to know, I had a fucking awful night, and now I'm having a fucking awful day.' He moved sideways so that Jane's hand fell from his arm, and made a slow detour around her.

Feeling bad about not recognizing Alan, Jane asks whether there's anything she can do.

'No.' He paused by the kitchen door: 'Well, maybe. You could help me off with my shoes. It just about kills me to bend over. And if you're going upstairs, you could bring down my pillows.'

'Yes, of course.' It occurred to Jane for the first time that there was a pattern here. Lately, Alan refused any offer of assistance at first, but soon corrected himself, asking for various objects and services. On other occasions he would wait longer, until she was somewhere else in the house and in the middle of some other activity, and then he would call for help.

'I can't go on like this. It's worse every day,' he muttered, leaning over the kitchen sink, gulping water and pills. He wiped his mouth on the cuff of his shirt, which should have been thrown in the laundry basket two days ago.

'I'm so sorry.' Jane put her arms around the soiled shirt and began a hug – but Alan winced, and she let go. 'Sorry,' she repeated.

As she helps him settle on the sofa and takes off his shoes, she thinks of what has happened, and she then goes to get his pillows.

> *Jane stood up. Who is this man lying on our sofa? she thought as she looked down on him. He's still called Alan Mackenzie, but he's not the same person. And I'm not the same person either, she thought as she climbed the stairs. I'm tired and worried and no fun for anybody, including myself. In a way we're not really husband and wife any more. We're housekeeper and employer. Or maybe, in the language of a blandly instructive pamphlet she had read while waiting for Alan in some doctor's office, caregiver and caregetter.*

Further on, reflecting on the changes in Alan, Jane recalls those books she read as a child in which selfish girls having had an accident are confined to bed for months, their suffering maturing them, giving them better characters.

> *But Alan hadn't needed to change for the better, Jane thought: he had been perfect as he was. So, logically, he had begun to change for the worse. His admirable evenness of temper, optimism and generosity of spirit had slowly begun to leak away. He had become overweight and unattractive, he had become self-centered and touchy.*
>
> *Those books were wrong, Jane thought. Pain is bad for the character, just as all misfortunes are: poverty and unemployment and loss of friends and family. It makes you tired and weak; it makes you depressed and anxious and fearful. Nobody says this, nobody is supposed to say it, but it is true. Even Jane herself, who was only forty and healthy and strong and attractive, would one day be old and tired and ugly and probably self-centered and touchy as well.*

Just about every sentence of this extract refers to a character in change. And the changes in Alan's character have caused a change in Jane's character. Moreover, these changes mean that further changes must occur, in that the book opens with such an intense, essentially double, conflict of character.

Write an opening showing the condition of change

Write the opening of a short story (250–300 words) narrated by a character in which she/he first notices a change in her partner/ friend/spouse/child. This change should suggest the plot tension.

Another example of developed characters changing occurs in the opening of Claire Messud's novel *The Woman Upstairs* (2013).

> *How angry am I? You don't want to know. Nobody wants to know about that.*
>
> *I'm a good girl, I'm a nice girl, I'm a straight-A, strait laced, good daughter, good career girl, and I never stole anybody's boyfriend and I never ran out on a girlfriend, and I put up with my parent's shit and my brother's shit, and I'm not a girl anyhow, I'm over forty fucking years old, and I'm good at my job and I'm great with kids and I held my mother's hand when she died, after four years of holding her hand while she was dying, and I speak to my father every day on the telephone – every day, mind you, and what kind of weather do you have on your side of the river, because here it's pretty gray and a bit muggy too? It was supposed to say 'Great Artist' on my tombstone, but if I died right now it would say 'such a good teacher/daughter/friend' instead; and what I really want to shout, and want in big letters on that grave, too, is FUCK YOU ALL.*
>
> *Don't all women feel the same? The only difference is how much we know we feel it, how in touch we are with our fury. We're all furies, except the ones who are too damned foolish, and my worry now is that we're brainwashing them from the cradle, and in the end even the ones who are smart will be too damned foolish. What do I mean? I mean the second graders at Appleton Elementary, sometimes the first graders even, and by the time they get to my classroom, to the third grade, they're well and truly gone – they're full of Lady Gaga and Katy Perry and French manicures and cute outfits and they care how*

their hair looks! In the third grade. They care more about their hair or their shoes than about galaxies or caterpillars or hieroglyphics. How did all that revolutionary talk of the seventies land us in a place where being female means playing dumb and looking good? Even worse on your tombstone than 'dutiful daughter' is 'looked good'; everyone used to know that. But we're lost in a world of appearances now.

That's why I'm so angry, really – not because of all the chores and all the making nice and all the duty of being a woman – or rather, of being me – because maybe these are the burdens of being human. Really I'm angry because I've tried so hard to get out of the hall of mirrors, this sham and pretend of the world, or of my world, on the East Coast of the United States of America in the first decade of the twenty-first century. And behind every mirror is another fucking mirror, and down every corridor is another corridor, and the Fun House isn't fun anymore and it isn't funny but there doesn't seem to be a door marked EXIT. ...

I'm not crazy. Angry, yes; crazy, no. My name is Nora Marie Eldridge and I'm forty-two years old – which is a lot more like middle age than forty or even forty-one. Neither old nor young, I'm neither fat nor thin, tall nor short, blond nor brunette, neither pretty nor plain. Quite nice looking in some moments, I think is the consensus, rather like the heroines of Harlequin romances, read in quantity in my youth. I'm neither married nor divorced, but single. What they used to call a spinster, but don't anymore, because it implies that you're dried up, and none of us wants to be that. Until last summer, I taught third grade at Appleton Elementary School in Cambridge, Massachusetts, and maybe I'll go back and do it again, I just don't know. Maybe, instead, I'll set the world on fire. I just might. ...

...I'm not an Underground Woman, harboring resentment for my miseries against the rest of the world. Or rather, it's not that I'm not in some sense an Underground Woman – aren't we all, who have to cede and swerve and step aside, unacknowledged and unadmired and unthanked? Numerous in our twenties and thirties, we're

positively legion in our forties and fifties. But the world should understand, if the world gave a shit, that women like us are not underground. No Ralph Ellison basement full of lightbulbs for us; no Dostoyevskian metaphorical subterra. We're always upstairs. We're not the madwomen in the attic – they get lots of play, one way or another. We're the quiet woman at the end of the third-floor hallway, whose trash is always tidy, who smiles brightly in the stairwell with a cheerful greeting, and who, from behind closed doors, never makes a sound. In our lives of quiet desperation, the woman upstairs is who we are, with or without a goddamn tabby or lolloping Labrador, and not a soul registers that we are furious. We're completely invisible.

I thought it wasn't true, or not true of me, but I've learned I am no different at all. The question now is how to work it, how to use that invisibility, to make it burn. ...

As for being invisible, it makes things more real. You walk into a room where you are not, and you hear what people say, unguardedly; you watch how they move when they aren't with you. You see them without their masks, because suddenly you can see them anywhere. It may be painful to learn what happens when you're behind the arras, but then, please God, you know.

All these years, I was wrong, you see. Most people around me, too. And especially now that I've learned that I really am invisible, I need to stop wanting to fly. I want to stop needing to fly. I want it all to do over again; but also I don't. I want to make my nothingness count. Don't think it's impossible.

With Messud's opening, the change in character is not directly due to the change in another character. The focus is on the first-person narrator's awareness of a change in herself. However, it makes sense to assume that whatever has caused this change has involved her relations with the world, with other people, as opposed to, for instance, a physical change in her brain.

CONCEPTS OF ROUNDED CHARACTERIZATION

The similarities and differences in the concepts of characterization between the Lurie and Messud openings are worth considering.

Similarities

- Both openings are narrated from a woman's point of view.
- Both openings present the character facing a problem.
- Both problems involve relationships.
- Both problems are existentially important.
- Both women are at a crisis.
- The crisis is a very unstable situation that will make something happen next – produce plot mechanisms – for the novels.
- Both characters are middle-class Americans.
- Both characters are in their early forties.
- Both are good-looking: 'attractive' in Lurie, 'nice looking' in Messud.

Significant differences

- Lurie writes in the third person of limited omniscience from her character Jane's point of view. This helps create a fairly objective tone.
- Messud writes in the first person. Nora speaks directly about herself. The tone is subjective.
- Jane's problems are presented with feeling, but with relative calm and common sense.
- Nora presents herself enraged, in a rant.
- The origin of Jane's problem is specifically explained, both in its source (Alan hurting his back) and in the shock of not recognizing him physically or temperamentally, forcing her to take stock of their relationship.
- Nora does not tell us exactly what/who has brought on her crisis. Instead, there's a socio-political content to her complaint, which gives her outrage context *as a woman* at a particular time and place in her life.
- Jane's thinking is not particularly allusive, except to a medical pamphlet and a moralistic type of children's story.
- Nora's allusions range from Lady Gaga and Harlequin romances to Ralph Ellison (*Invisible Man*) and Dostoyevsky (*Notes from the Underground* and other writing), and there are at least two well-known references implied in 'We're not the mad woman in the attic.'

As writers, what is even more important for us to consider when reading these two openings of novels, in which fully developed characters are introduced, is what holds our attention and why we want to read on.

In the Lurie novel, this is fairly obvious. The realistically detailed setting, the character in her particular context, the details of her relationship and the 'solving' of the initial puzzle of why she fails to recognize her own husband pique your story interest as well as give you enough dialogue and imagery to hear and picture the scene in your own imagination. More, the other characters mentioned – the property tax inspector, the FBI official and the 'half-threatening' guy – help produce a lively human depth to Jane's character. Finally, Jane's thoughts about her relationship with Alan raise our expectations of further developments in this tense relationship in which both characters are changing.

By contrast, the Messud opening has no other specific character (a dead mother and living father and brother are not really in this scene). There is no physical action (except for an ironically clichéd phone conversation); nor is there imagery of any setting. Nora is only a talking head. There's no idea of plot, since we don't know anything of what or who has caused her crisis. There is the problem of women's position in life, but you'll have come across this many times before and it remains unlinked to her particular rage. Even her promises to do something about it, something drastic, are so unspecified as to create no particular expectations for what may follow in the book. So why should you read on? Yet read on you want to do.

Characterization and language

It's the language drama Messud gives Nora, it's the sound, its words and its wordplay and its rhythmic repetitions that hold you and hold the promise of more.

The short opening paragraph catches you with the first of a number of shifts in meaning. In 'How angry am I? You don't want to know', the second sentence is the colloquial paradox meaning something like, 'hugely angry' or even 'so angry that you're dying to hear'. But this is followed by 'Nobody wants to know about *that*', making the original colloquialism literal rather than ironic, merely an empty convention, much as the casual question 'How are you?' isn't generally expected to be answered with 'My father has broken his hip and my sister's alcoholism is destroying her family.'

And then you're swept up into the next paragraph's dazzle of parallelism. 'I'm a good girl, I'm a nice girl.' Then an assonant homonym pair: 'I'm a straight-A, strait laced'; then 'good' comes in again in 'good daughter, good career girl' (which repeats 'girl'). This is followed by the two 'and I never', and that by 'my parents' shit and my brother's shit' and it rolls on to pick up 'girl' again but then contradicts it with 'and I'm not a girl anyhow', underlining it with the alliteration of 'I'm over forty fucking years old'. From here, it slows pace in order to build to a crescendo of rage: 'but if I died right now it [her tombstone] would say "such a good teacher/daughter/friend"; and what I really want to shout, and want in big letters on that grave, too is' – and then the mimetic shout – 'FUCK YOU ALL.'

This is a song of despair *con brio*. No wonder you want to read on. And the rest of this opening continues as variations on these sound and rhyme themes, the harsh music of Nora's mind carrying its thoughts and emotions to keep you reading. And as you come to see when you read the book, it's not for nothing that Nora shares her name with the central character of Ibsen's *A Doll's House*.

So here are two openings of novels with fully developed characters. The differences between them clearly indicate there is no single or any best way to develop characters in depth.

Edit exercise

Take any of your character narrators and rewrite his/her opening narration so that the language grabs hold of the reader (about 500 words).

Write two opening scenes

Write two 300–400-word openings of a piece of fiction, novel or short story. The material can be new for this exercise or a reworking of writing in your portfolio.

The first piece, like the Lurie opening, is to involve a scene with two main characters in a relationship and should be narrated in the third person, past tense, limited omniscience from the point of view of one of the characters.

The second piece, like the Messud opening, should be narrated in first person, present tense, and not involve another character in a major way, though it can refer to people other than the speaker. As with the Messud opening, it should focus on language rather than action or dialogue to hold reader interest.

Rounded characters in the short story

It's obvious that the novel, in its length, offers the space for in-depth character development. There's the opportunity for more scenes, longer scenes, more action, dialogue, interaction and introspection than in a short story. The range and number of characters possible in a novel means that central characters can be observed and reflected through a number of different points of view.

Since short stories – which I'm limiting for this argument to lengths between 2,000 and 20,000 words – don't have the novel's space for such types of development, how can they develop character in depth? They can, first, by usually limiting main characters to between one and three. Then, timeframes are typically short. When they're not, there are big jumps forward or backward in time. Finally, something happens that is either of great importance to the main character(s) or is of great importance to the reader's understanding of the character(s).

 Key idea

The best short stories, noisy or quiet, are revelations of character – of those in the story and/or in the reader.

ACTION AND CHARACTER DEVELOPMENT

The central character of the short story **'Hurricanes Anonymous'**, by Adam Johnson (2009), is called Nonc, his girlfriend Relle's name for him rather than his real name, Randall. Relle has told him that it's easier to understand for Nonc's toddler son Geronimo, whom Nonc and Relle call G, or G-ron or G-man. The boy got his name when Nonc's ex, Marnie, told him she was pregnant and he said Geronimo, 'in that fuck-it way, like someone jumping from a plane', only Marnie took it in 'a birth certificate way'.

That's some indication of the social level in which the story takes place. The setting is Louisiana, just after Hurricane Katrina, when Nonc is driving for UPS and living in the van with Geronimo, except when Relle is in there with him while old ladies babysit Geronimo at an AA meeting he and Relle have had to join so they can sneak out together to the van while the boy is being looked after. Nonc has had the baby since the day after Hurricane Katrina, when he waded back to the van to find Geronimo in there with 'a yellow boom box and a bag of clothes', and not even a note.

Nonc, Geronimo and Relle are the fixed and driving points of the story. Here's its opening paragraph:

> *Nonc pulls up outside Chuck E. Cheese's and hits the hazards on his UPS van. The last working cell tower in Lake Charles, Louisiana, is not far away, so he stops here a couple of times a day to check his messages. He turns to his son, who's strapped into a bouncy chair rigged from cargo hooks, and attempts to snag his cell from the boy, a two-and-a-half-year-old named Geronimo.*

Look at the sheer amount of exposition in these sentences: names of characters, relationships, work, location, specific detail ('bouncy chair rigged from cargo hooks'), and in 'last working cell tower' the significant timeframe of the story (coupled with the 'Hurricanes' of the title). Yet this reads coherently and not like some list of facts and it keeps the focus on character in action, the action also vivid through colloquial verbs like 'hits' and 'snag'.

An opening paragraph like this rarely comes word-perfect in the first draft of your writing. It is too knowing about many levels of the story's details and its main characters not to be to some real extent composed/revised in retrospect. (If I'm wrong about this, Adam Johnson is one rare writer.)

Key idea

Perfectly pitched opening sentences in fiction that give a great deal of exposition and characterization are generally arrived at through redrafting and editing.

When you bring a little child or a mom who's poorly or any kind of puppy into a piece of fiction, you always have to try to avoid the potential for sentimentality; that is, the dependence on automatic reader reaction to certain stereotypes rather than on real sentiment created by the writing. Here are some of the ways Johnson avoids this.

He follows the opening paragraph with:

> *'Eyeball,' Geronimo says into the phone. 'Eyeball.'*
> *It's one of the boy's few words, and Nonc has no idea what*
> *it means.*
>
> *'Trade?' Nonc asks as he raises a sippy cup of chocolate*
> *milk. 'For some gla-gla?'*
> *Geronimo has puffy little-boy eyes, white nubbly teeth, and*
> *an unfortunate sunburn.*

The boy is here characterized as slow in language (at two-and-a-half) and not a lovely-looking child; the 'unfortunate sunburn' is pitiable but nonetheless unattractive.

It's critical that Johnson avoid sentimentality with the child, since the story's central conflict is that within Nonc and between Nonc and Relle to keep on literally caring for the child, as Relle works to make him care less. You can see this in Relle's renaming of Randall to Nonc, ostensibly to make it easier for the toddler to say his name. But 'Nonc' is a Cajun contraction of 'mon oncle', and an uncle, however friendly, is not a father. At one point, Relle sticks swab sticks into Nonc and Geronimo's mouths to get the free DNA tests in the hurricane's aftermath to help reunite seperated families, Relle's hope being that it could help disunite her lover from the child.

But the struggle is rarely this overt. For one thing, Relle is mostly too canny to reveal her true motives to Nonc. For another, Johnson makes Nonc immature and easy-going enough to want his freedom, as in the following scene when he delivers a package. Nonc has asked directions from a man in a cherry-picker, working to restore the power. He's directed Nonc out to the end of a dock.

> *With a folding knife, he unwraps Snyder's Guide to the*
> *Birds of the Gulf Wetlands.*
>
> *'People mostly shoot at birds around here,' Nonc says.*
>
> *Geronimo holds up the DIAD, and the engineer takes*
> *notice of him, pulls off his hat. With his hand, like a*
> *puppeteer, he makes the floppy hat talk like Yoda. 'A*
> *signature is wanted, hmm?' the hat asks. 'And here we have*
> *what, hmm, a child, a boy child, have we, yes?'*
> *Geronimo nears the hat and stares into its folds as if trying*
> *to determine its intentions.*

Yoda scrutinizes his face. 'Serious, this one is, hmm. Much turmoil has he seen.' The engineer glances at Nonc for confirmation. 'All around is uncertainty.' The puppet looks up and down the street, but Geronimo doesn't follow. 'Broken are many things, yes, and not in their proper places.' Vollman has the puppet take the stylus and, mumbling as if its mouth were too full to talk, sign the DIAD. That gets a laugh.

'Got a boy exactly his age,' Vollman says. 'Two kids off to college, and then along comes Henry.'

'Cajuns call that lagniappe,' Nonc says. 'It means getting more than you were bargaining for.'

'I tell you,' Vollman says, tousling Geronimo's hair. 'It sure is hard to leave them.'

Nonc has tried to imagine that moment Marnie put the boy in the van – if only he could think of what she said to him when she left, maybe he'd know where she went, when she might be coming back for him.

'What did you tell him,' Nonc asks, 'you know, when you left?'

'Henry?'

'Yeah.'

'I said, "I'll be right back." Kids this age, they don't understand time. They don't know what a month is. Plus, they don't remember. I made some mistakes, parentwise, believe me. At this age, you got some wiggle room.'

'This is all just temporary,' Nonc says. 'The boy's going back with his mama soon.'

'The hurricane turned some lives upside down,' Vollman says. 'Obviously you two are in some sort of situation, but seriously, the boy can't be running around in his jammies. Look at the glass and nails. He needs some boots and jeans, something.'

The pajamas are actually a custom tracksuit that Relle made for the boy, but Nonc doesn't say anything.

Even in such a long short story as this – about 15,000 words – it's tautological to say that this is an important scene, but it is a good example of the use of a minor character in developing a major character. First, note that Vollman is himself a developed character. The character in the cherry-picker is absolutely flat, existing only as part of the work scene in which electricity is being reinstated and to point Nonc to Vollman who sits on the 'only surviving dock, reading blueprints'.

Vollman's appearance is individualistic, out of keeping with the work scene and its destruction. Nonc sees he's wearing some sort of floppy naturalist's hat ('a boonie-rat hat') and has 'serious binoculars'. When the package he delivers turns out to be a local bird guide, Nonc understands that Vollman is a bird watcher, and his comment, 'People mostly shoot at birds around here', suggests an ironic intelligence, in that this says nothing about whether the people manage to hit the birds. The statement also shows (not tells) Nonc's openness, curiosity and general friendliness.

As Vollman notices Geronimo, the scene moves into its main subject, the relation between fathers and sons. Vollman, with two college-age children and a surprising third, a boy the same age as Geronimo, takes on the role of older mentor with some sensitivity, noting in his Yoda-puppet voice Geronimo's, and to some extent Nonc's, psychological state.

But even as Vollman tells Nonc, 'tousling Geronimo's hair', that it's hard to leave his little boy to go to work, in answering Nonc's question about what he tells him – that 'I'll be right back' – Johnson sets up a situation in which Nonc can also decide to follow Vollman's comments about children this age not understanding about time. This 'wiggle room' can become Nonc's rationalization for abandoning his son, though Vollman is tactfully speaking about a father's responsibility to care.

Vollman has practical as well as moral/emotional advice for Nonc, pointing out 'but seriously, the boy can't be running around in his jammies. Look at the glass and nails. He needs some boots and jeans, something.' Something indeed. That Nonc's response is to silently correct Vollman about the pajamas actually being 'a custom tracksuit that Relle made for the boy' shows (not tells) the powerful hold Relle has on him. But his silence also shows Nonc's shame at his negligence regarding Geronimo.

This is Vollman's scene, but it's also entirely relevant to the development of Nonc's character in the story. The story-driving tension is how Nonc's dilemma will play out. Will he continue to take care of Geronimo, or will he, too, abandon the child?

Develop a major character through a minor character

Take one of your more developed characters, either one you've created for an exercise in this book or one from your portfolio, and write a 750-word scene in which you create a minor character interacting with your existing character so that the minor character is a real individual (developed character) while at the same time this scene consistently develops your major character.

EMOTION AND CHARACTER DEVELOPMENT

Like Adam Johnson's 'Hurricanes Anonymous', Joy William's short story **'Taking Care'** also concerns a parent, a mother who dumps a child, a baby girl. But this doesn't drive the story, because early on you're told that the two main characters, Jones the preacher and his dying wife, have been left with the baby while its mother, their daughter, goes off to Mexico because it's an astrological necessity.

You also learn early that Jones's wife is dying, so there's no will-she-won't-she tension there. Further, Jones looks after his wife and the baby and the dog, also left by the daughter, with unquestioning love and devotion. Moreover, the dying wife loves her husband and daughter and granddaughter, so, again, no driving tension for the plot. As for the daughter, when she writes to her father, she makes no mention of her baby, her mother or her dog. So the ordinary story concept of character-driven plot tension doesn't really exist here. Then how does one thing lead to another? And what are these 'things'?

Unlike many other writers, Joy Williams uses the most powerful human emotions, her 'things', around which to organize and propel the forward motion of her fiction. How she goes about pitting love against despair, and life and joy against suffering and meanness and death is what I'll try to indicate to you in looking at elements of her prose in this short story. On their own, emotions are abstractions, yet her writing is not abstract, though a character's thinking may be. Note: I'm trying to show you a way of creating deeply developed character, not, I repeat not, explaining the writer's internal creative process.

To begin with something obvious when you read 'Taking Care', one way the writing focuses on its central character, Jones, is that no other character, major or minor, is named. Nor is Jones even given a first name. Something else that's obvious is the absence of dialogue. There's some, but not much. You don't miss it because the third-person narration is so close to Jones's point of view that you tend to hear its thoughts as his voice. Also obvious is the larger organizing method. The story, about 4,500 words, is broken into ten long paragraphs and one final medium-length paragraph. Between each, there can be shifts from the present (in present-tense narration) into the past and back again.

But to look at character development, you have to look closer. Here's the opening of the story, about two-thirds of its first paragraph:

> *Jones, the preacher, has been in love all his life. He is baffled by this because as far as he can see, it has never helped anyone, even when they have acknowledged it, which is not often. Jones's love is much too apparent and arouses neglect. He is like an animal in a traveling show who, through some aberration, wears a vital organ outside the skin, awkward and unfortunate, something that shouldn't be seen, certainly something that shouldn't be watched working. Now he sits on a bed besides his wife in the self-care unit of a hospital fifteen miles from their home. She has been committed here for tests. She is so weak, so tired. There is something wrong with her blood. Her arms are covered with bruises where they have gone into the veins. Her hip, too, is blue and swollen where they have drawn out samples of bone marrow. All of this is frightening. The doctors are severe and wise, answering Jones's questions in a way that makes him feel hopelessly deaf. They have told him that there really is no such thing as a disease of the blood, for the blood is not a living tissue but a passive vehicle for the transportation of food, oxygen and waste. They have told him that abnormalities in the blood corpuscles, which his wife seems to have, must be regarded as symptoms of disease elsewhere in the body. They have shown him, upon request, slides and charts of normal and pathological blood cells which look to Jones like canapés. They speak (for he insists) of leukocytosis, myelocytes and megaloblasts. None of this takes into account the love he has for his wife.*

One device used for characterization here is not so complex. It comes immediately after 'Jones's love is much too apparent and arouses neglect' (note the originality and wonderful aptness of the active 'arouses' with the typically passive 'neglect'). It's the simile in 'He is like an animal in a traveling show who, through some aberration, wears a vital organ outside the skin, awkward and unfortunate, something that shouldn't be seen, certainly something that shouldn't be watched working.'

This, taken back to its cliché origin, would be merely 'Jones wears his heart on his sleeve'. But here the transformed cliché forces you to face the awful, off-putting human heart pumping away on a man's arm, and rather than marvel at seeing the heart in action, you're frightened and revolted by its nakedness and choose to look away. The particular imagery is original to Williams, but the linguistic device of transforming a 'trite but true' statement into a striking one by making its figurative language literal is well known, though seen more in poetry than prose.

More complex is something I'll call the rhythm or patterning of emotional opposites in the sequence of paragraph sentences quoted above. It works like this: if you look at the first sentence ('Jones, the preacher...') on its own, you'd say its emotional meaning or tone was positive. If you did this with the second sentence ('He is baffled...'), you'd say it was negative. The third sentence ('Jones's love is much too apparent...') is first positive and then negative. Then comes the emotionally negative transformed cliché sentence. The one after that ('Now he sits on a beds beside his wife...') is positive in arousing our sympathy. The next one, 'She has been committed here for tests,' is terribly negative, with 'committed' suggesting a sentence passed on her, almost as if she is guilty of her illness, a word of Kafkaesque intensity. The next sentence, 'She is so tired, so weak,' again engages your sympathy, and the one after that ('There is something wrong...'), though in itself neutral in tone, partakes of the prior sentence's sympathy. But the following two sentences describing the visible physical effects of her tests are made intensely, almost hatefully negative. The first describes the bruising on her arm 'where they have gone into the veins'; the second the bruising on her hip 'where they have drawn out samples of blood marrow'. The impersonal 'they' is chilling. These might be statements describing Mengele at work.

What propels this writing is not the tension produced between characters but tension from the repeated positive–negative content and tone, the tension between the pity and terror it invokes in you, though on this scale you don't experience their catharsis.

Another distinctive feature of this prose and of its way of characterization is that it often proceeds not so much by a linear as by an associative coherence. Consider the following excerpt that occurs as Jones listens to a recording of a work he's never heard before, Mahler's *Kindertotenlieder* (Songs of Dead Children). He's struggling to understand the lyrics, hampered by having studied only technical German many years ago in college.

> *These lessons are neither of life or death. Why was he instructed in them? In the hospital, his wife waits to be translated, no longer a woman, the woman whom he loves, but a situation. Her blood moves mysteriously as constellations. She is under scrutiny and attack and she has abandoned Jones. She is a swimmer waiting to get on with the drowning. Jones is on the shore. In Mexico, his daughter walks along the beach with two men. She is acting out a play that has become her life. Jones is on the mountaintop. The baby cries and Jones takes her from the crib to change her. The dog paws the door. Jones lets him out. He settles down with the baby and listens to the record. He still cannot make out many of the words. The baby wriggles restlessly on his lap. Her eyes are foal's eyes, navy-blue. She has grown in a few weeks to expect everything from Jones. He props her on one edge of the couch and goes to her small toy box where he keeps a bear, a few rattles and balls. On the way, he opens the door and the dog immediately enters. His heavy coat is fragrant with ice. He noses the baby and she squeals.*
>
> Oft denk'ich, sie sind nur ausgegangen
> Bald werden sie wieder nach Hause gelangen
>
> *Jones selects a bright ball and pushes it gently in her direction.*

This is a version of the associations. Jones first wonders why he should have studied technical German ('neither of life or death') rather than the spoken, living language. This leads him to think of his sick wife who 'waits to be translated'. As Jones tries to translate the German lyrics, he thinks of his wife being translated from life to death, from the woman he loves into medical data ('a situation'). The data is about her blood, which 'moves mysteriously as constellations'. Here he recalls what the doctors have told him about blood, about it being the body's carrier or mover. Jones's anger at this cruel 'translation' of his wife is expressed as her being 'under scrutiny and attack'. The blood will carry his wife away from him, so she becomes 'a swimmer waiting to get on with the drowning' while he is left, helplessly, watching from the shore.

What at first seems a jump to his daughter in Mexico, in the following sentence is an association of his daughter also being away from him and his wife's blood, that 'carrier' away, moving 'mysteriously as constellations', the reference to 'heavens' linking to his daughter's astrologically driven travels. Jones sees his daughter, like himself, on the shore as 'she walks along the beach with two men', an image of her promiscuity. To Jones, her careless life seems unreal, as if 'she is acting out a play that has become her life'. He can observe her clearly because he is now 'on the mountaintop', associated with the place of his daughter's star-predicted breakdown.

Such associative sequencing has the logic of dreams and this is literally what is happening: a half-waking, half-dozing, as Jones listens to the music.

At this point the baby cries, waking Jones, so the writing shifts into clear, simple prose, the prose of doing, of action, of everyday caring. He changes the baby, he lets out the dog, he sits on the couch with the baby and again listens to the record, not able to make out many words. The baby wriggles and he sets her up on the couch to get her a toy. On the way he opens the door and the dog comes in and 'noses' the baby and she squeals, and the writing has the tact not to tell you what you feel, what you know – that the squeal is of delight and love.

All of this, the dreaming, the waking and doing, is an intense development of character, an insistent, deep showing, not telling, of character.

And then, you, too, hear the lyrics, the two lines of German, which you understand or don't or struggle to understand. They translate as, 'I often think they have just gone out / And will soon come home again.' But since the living child is really there, 'Jones selects a bright ball and pushes it gently in her direction.'

This excerpt is a vividly dramatic rendering of a suffering, wondering, caring person, in other words someone fully human, and it ends with the transcendence of a 'bright ball' pushed 'gently' towards the child.

One of the story's long paragraph sections is a single country scene as Jones and his granddaughter drive along in the first snow of the season. This begins as a scene of transcendence, when the beauty of the woods and fields and Jones's enjoyment of the baby's interest peaks in the sight of a white hare running across the snow, and Jones, despite his wife's mortal illness and his daughter's fecklessness, feels joy. But such triumph over despair comes to nothing when the scene becomes horrible. Yet transcendence remains a possibility.

Despite the dying and the daughter walking through the story like a beloved curse, there is humour here, and the humour has wit. Early on, you find it in 'Jones's daughter has fallen in with the stars and is using the heavens, as Jones would be the first to admit, more than he ever has.' 'Fallen in with' is rich: it is indeed a fall away from personal responsibility, from taking care, and in another sense she is indeed marching along under the command of astrology. And even in the story's opening paragraph, in Jones's attempt to learn everything about his wife's illness, he asks to see normal and pathological images of 'blood cells which look to Jones like canapés'. This is not cold, gallows humour; it's the realistic comparison which tries, but fails, to somehow, any way, cling to a disappearing feeling of normality and hope. You're reminded of the Irish saying, 'The situation's hopeless, but not serious.' Or later, after a tender description of Jones feeding the baby, she's able to hold the spoon and 'sometimes turns it around and puts the wrong end into her mouth', there comes 'Of course, there is nothing that cannot be done incorrectly.' Mordant, maybe, but certainly a funny truism.

The concept of transcendence is very much worth thinking about in a discussion about creating great depth of character. At an obvious level, this is a story about Jones the preacher, so religious allusion makes sense. But it's more than surface realism. Here is the story's last paragraph. It takes place after Jones's wife has been diagnosed with the cancer that – as she's known from the start – is killing her.

For insurance purpose, Jones's wife is brought out to the car in a wheelchair. She is thin and beautiful. Jones is grateful and confused. He has a mad wish to tip the orderly. Have so many years really passed? Is this not his wife, his love, fresh from giving birth? Isn't everything about to begin? In Mexico, his daughter wanders disinterestedly through a jewelry shop where she picks up a small silver egg. It opens on a hinge and inside are two figures, a bride and groom. Jones puts the baby in his wife's arms. At first the baby is alarmed because she cannot remember this person very well and she reaches for Jones, whimpering. But soon she is soothed by his wife's soft voice and she falls asleep in her arms as they drive. Jones has readied everything carefully for his wife's homecoming. The house is clean and orderly. For days he has restricted himself to only one part of the house so that his clutter will be minimal. Jones helps his wife up the steps to the door. Together they enter the shining rooms.

One after another, the sequence of associated sentences is clear and hard and moving. There is the kindness of the hospital providing a wheelchair to avoid lawsuits. Jones is so relieved to have her back again that he wishes to tip the orderly, as if she were coming out of a hotel, as if she and everything were good again. Yet as he sees her he knows how time has passed and he is confused. Aren't they bringing their own baby daughter back from the hospital after her birth? Their daughter in Mexico looks into an egg without feeling; it gives birth to a bride and groom, maybe the husband she's left, maybe her parents – it doesn't matter. What matters is that the baby's whimpering is soothed by his dying wife's gentle voice, and she sleeps in her arms. They come, finally, to the door of their home, which Jones has meticulously prepared. He helps her, as he would his bride. They enter and there is, for a moment, transcendence – no death, no loss, no horror – only the pure light, only love.

This is an original and profound way of creating fully developed characters. At this level, story and image, thought and action, despair and hope and the complexity of being work together. You can learn from this.

Revitalize the cliché

We are all familiar with clichés like 'she's a pretty picture', 'he's devilishly handsome', 'he's the strong, silent type', 'she's cool as a cucumber', 'a stitch in time saves nine', 'handsome is as handsome does', and so on. The list of such expressions is, alas, very long, but they're all so overused that they really don't get reader attention; they switch it off.

Write 350–500 words making a clichéd expression new. Apply it to one of your own characters. (Model this on the Joy Williams example above.)

Workshop

For this workshop, take what you consider to be a major and/or important piece of fiction from your portfolio. Consider each of the following statements about character and apply it critically (which can be positively as well as negatively) to the characters in that piece of fiction.

- Even the flattest character has to be functional; that is, it must serve a purpose.
- There are times when it's difficult to say with certainty whether a character is essentially rounded or flat. (The example of the three main characters in 'The Comforts of Home' is a case in point.)
- Non-linear or associative character development can be a powerful method of character development.
- Characters can be powerfully developed by showing, rather than by telling.
- Particular, original language helps make characterization memorable.
- From the chapters on character types, which of these writers do you think your character development is most like – Flannery O'Connor, James Joyce, Alison Lurie, Claire Messud, Adam Johnson or Joy Williams?
- Which of these writers do you wish your character development was like?
- Why, in particular?

Focus points

- When a novel or short story opens, it often establishes the conditions of fully developed characters, especially the condition of *change*. The change in character may or may not be due to the change in another character.
- Depth of character sparking interest in the reader may be created through setting, the character in relationship to others or the 'solving' of a puzzle. It may also come about through the use of language – its sound, its words and its wordplay and its rhythms.
- Action and conflict as well as showing deep emotion are all ways of developing powerful, fully rounded characters that have a profound impact on the reader.

Next step

In the next chapter, you'll be looking at how different types of narration and points of view are determinants of character, both for the narrative voice and the other characters narrated.

4

Narration and character

The context of fictional narration affects what a reader makes of its characters.

For example, Joseph Conrad used the context in which his stories were told as an active element of characterization. Famously, in *Heart of Darkness,* the misery and savagery of the story of colonial exploitation in 'deepest' Africa is given ironic resonance by its being told, narrated, among a group of British businessmen sitting on a yacht moored in the Thames, in the heart of London, the heart of empire, at the heart of the 'heart of darkness'.

Narrative context and character

You can see the contextual effect on character at work in detail in Conrad's First World War story 'The Tale', written in 1916. The following extract opens the story. It is followed by a summary of the story – 'the tale' of the title – and then another extract, of the final part. Here's the opening:

Outside the large single window the crepuscular light was dying out slowly in a great square gleam, without colour, framed rigidly in the gathering shades of the room.

It was a long room. The irresistible tide of the night ran into the most distant part of it, where the whispering of the man's voice, passionately interrupted and passionately renewed, seemed to plead against the answering murmurs of infinite sadness.

At last no answering murmur came. His movement when he rose slowly from his knees by the side of the deep, shadowy couch holding the shadowy suggestion of a reclining woman revealed him tall under the low ceiling, and sombre all over except for the crude discord of the white collar under the shape of his head and the faint, minute spark of a brass button here and there on his uniform.

He stood over her a moment, masculine and mysterious in his immobility, before he sat down on a chair near by. He could see only the faint oval of her upturned face and, extended on her black dress, her pale hands, a moment before abandoned to his kisses and now as if too weary to move.

He dared not make a sound, shrinking as a man would do from the prosaic necessities of existence. As usual, it was the woman who had the courage. Her voice was heard first – almost conventional while her being vibrated yet with conflicting emotions.

'Tell me something,' she said.

The darkness hid his surprise and then his smile. Had he not just said to her everything worth saying in the world – and that not for the first time!

'What am I to tell you?' he asked, in a voice creditably steady. He was beginning to feel grateful to her for that something final in her tone which had eased the strain.

'Why not tell me a tale?'

'A tale!' He was really amazed.

'Yes. Why not?'

These words came with a slight petulance, the hint of a loved woman's capricious will, which is capricious only because it feels itself to be a law, embarrassing sometimes and always difficult to elude.

'Why not?' he repeated, with a slightly mocking accent, as though he had been asked to give her the moon. But now he was feeling a little angry with her for that feminine mobility that slips out of an emotion as easily as out of a splendid gown. He heard her say, a little unsteadily with a sort of fluttering intonation which made him think suddenly of a butterfly's flight:

'You used to tell – your – your simple and – and professional – tales very well at one time. Or well enough to interest me. You had a – a sort of art – in the days – the days before the war.'

And before he tells her a tale, a tale of the war he's in, he says in response to her suggestion that 'It could be a tale not of this world':

'…But you forget that I have only five days' leave.'

'Yes. And I've also taken a five days leave from – from my duties.'

'I like that word.'

'What word?'

'Duty.'

'It is horrible – sometimes.'

'Oh, that's because you think it's narrow. But it isn't. It contains infinities, and – and so…'

'What is this jargon?'

He disregarded the interjected scorn. 'An infinity of absolution, for instance,' he continued. 'But as to this "another world" – who's going to look for it and for that tale that is in it?'

'You,' she said, with a strange, almost rough, sweetness of assertion.

He made a shadowy movement of assent in his chair, the irony of which not even the gathered darkness could render mysterious.

'As you will. In that world, then, there was once upon a time a Commanding Officer and a Northman. Put in the capitals, please, because they had no other names.'

The above excerpt introduces this tale, which, with a few interjections from the woman who listens, takes up the bulk of the story. The man then tells the tale of the Commanding Officer patrolling a fogbound coast, looking to intercept any shipping carrying arms to the enemy. The Commanding Officer, you know, is himself, and the Northman is master of a cargo boat he intercepts, a ship out of a neutral Nordic country.

In this tale, the Northman tells the Officer his own tale of getting completely lost in day after day of fog, and of not knowing this coast at all. Although the Officer's men have searched the ship and found nothing suspicious, the Officer knows the Northman had his engines running just before he heard the Officer's ship approaching, but he tells the Officer that he's been stopped at anchor while trying to figure out the charts. To the Officer, this indicates that the Northman was keeping silence, hoping the Officer's ship would pass without noticing them. So the Northman has something to hide, he thinks, even though they haven't been able to locate whatever it is. A cat and mouse game is played in which the Officer won't accuse the Northman and the Northman, increasingly nervous, won't deviate from his story.

Finally, the Officer gives the Northman an exact course to take in order to avoid the dangerous rocks. At this, the Northman asks, 'Must I? What could induce me? I haven't the nerve.' The Officer replies, 'And yet you must go. Unless you want to…' He leaves the word 'confess' or 'surrender' unspoken. The Northman says he doesn't want to, says he's had enough of this game. The Officer returns to his ship and tells his officers merely that he's let the cargo ship go.

Conrad's story ends with this:

> *The narrator bent forward towards the couch, where no movement betrayed the presence of a living person.*
>
> *'Listen,' he said forcibly. 'That course would lead the Northman straight on a deadly ledge of rock. And the Commanding Officer gave it to him. He steamed out – ran on it – and went down. So he had spoken the truth. He did not know where he was. But it proves nothing. Nothing either way. It may have been the only truth in all his story. And yet... He seems to have been driven out by a menacing stare – nothing more.'*
>
> *He abandoned all pretence.*
>
> *'Yes, I gave that course to him. It seemed to me a supreme test. I believe – no, I don't believe. I don't know. At the time I was certain. They all went down; and I don't know whether I have done stern retribution – or murder; whether I have added to the corpses that litter the bed of the unreadable sea the bodies of men completely innocent or basely guilty. I don't know. I shall never know.'*
>
> *He rose. The woman on the couch got up and threw her arms around his neck. Her eyes put two gleams in the deep shadow of the room. She knew his passion for truth, his horror of deceit, his humanity.*
>
> *'Oh, my poor, poor...'*
>
> *'I shall never know,' he repeated, sternly, disengaged himself, pressed her hands to his lips, and went off.*

This story, then, consists of a 'present' scene (in omniscient past-tense narration) between a man and a woman in which the man narrates a 'tale'. The tale he tells takes up the bulk of the story, and he tells it in the third person. Though he admits in the end that he was its chief character, you understand this from the start. You also know that the woman knows he's speaking about himself from the start. And since you also know that the man knows from the start that the woman will know this, and since there are no military secrets given away, you understand that the man has a psychological need to distance himself from the events he narrates, though he can't, in the end, keep up the pretence.

The man–woman scene opening and closing Conrad's story is sometimes called a **framing device**, in that it surrounds and sets off the story told within. 'Sets off' also means it contextualizes that central story (as it does in Conrad's *Heart of Darkness*).

One way to approach what's happening in 'The Tale' is first to imagine that there's no framing device, no special contextualization. The tale narrated on its own might change, to the extent of giving the Officer a name, or it could be narrated by the Officer, named or not, in the first person. Either way, what you'd get is a war story of possible deceit or double deceit in which, despite the Officer's best judgement at the time, he can never be certain of the truth and therefore the justice of his decision to send the freighter and all aboard it to destruction. In the hands of a writer as good as Conrad, it could be a good, gripping story in itself, a story of psychological and moral depth. But it wouldn't at all be the story that Conrad wrote.

The story opens in fading light – though not sunset: the longer, slower 'crepuscular light was dying out slowly', a light 'without colour', and away from the window are 'the gathering shades of the room'. The darkening is 'the irresistible tide of the night'. Conrad then slowly moves you into the shadows in which you first hear, rather than see, the people 'whispering' and 'in murmurs ... passionately interrupted and passionately renewed'.

Visually, the characters are revealed not clearly but in 'shadowy suggestion' and, aside from a gleam or two, there's little clarity about their features. There is an indistinctness, a hidden quality to this scene, a common enough scene of lovemaking, of a man and woman in love. Yet the hush and failing light suggest that 'hidden' could apply to more than the setting.

As the characters begin to speak, the dialogue reveals that they have been lovers for some time. He used to tell her tales, 'professional ... tales' in 'the days before the war'. Conrad's perceptive narration of the differences between the man and the woman's psychological and emotional reactions to the end of their lovemaking keeps you interested in these two. It's also clear that much is understood between them without needing to be spoken.

As they talk and tease, almost flirtatiously, about the subject of the tale she wants from him, he reminds her that 'I have only five days leave.' She replies, 'Yes. And I've also taken a five days' leave from – from my duties.'

Suddenly you know. You may have suspected, given the setting, but now you know that these are illicit, adulterous lovers. His leave is literal, since you know he's military (the 'minute spark of a brass button here and there on his uniform'). Hers is a euphemism for five days away from husband and, likely, family, to be with him.

As a military man, he appreciates her use of the word 'duty', but she thinks it 'horrible', and immediately catches herself to add 'sometimes', meaning especially now that she's with her lover. But when the officer begins to think of his 'duties' in the abstract, the woman becomes unhappy and asks what he is actually talking about. His response is that her 'duties' contain 'An infinity of absolution'. He says this as a gentleman lover must, gallantly, though this could in reality be his rationale, for of course he could not love her if she were merely unfaithful, merely an adulteress. It is an understandable self-deceit.

Then comes the tale, a tale of fog and shadow, of deceit played for life or death stakes, pursued under the pressure of war's essentially immoral logic. And after he tells his war tale, she understands his suffering and throws her arms around him. 'She knew his passion for truth, his horror of deceit, his humanity.' And when she says, 'Oh, my poor, poor…' he simply cannot stand the pity and leaves: he feels too strongly the irony she may be able to suppress.

The story's framing not only mirrors and reinforces the 'tale's' shadowy, ambiguous conflicts, but it also calls into question, through its intense ironies, the morality both the man and the woman profess the other possesses. So their 'passion for truth' and 'horror of deceit' are deeply compromised. What you feel is definitely not compromised is their 'humanity'. You feel you have looked deeply into the human condition. They are, you feel, deeply in love, for which you, too, ironically forgive them almost everything.

 ## Edit exercise

Taking a story or a novel from your portfolio, write a framing scene (i.e. opening and closing scene) of about one thousand words in total which somewhat changes – deepens or makes more ambiguous or ironically revealing – the fiction framed. Have the opening scene be longer than the ending scene.

 ## Key idea

Differences in narrative person, tense and point of view alter the tone, the significance and the meaning of character presentation and development.

To illustrate the above key idea, read the following brief statements introducing the same character.

1 Valerie Richards was a beautiful young woman, shy, and often in trouble. Generally, the trouble was not of her making.

2 I always felt sorry for Valerie Richards. When young, she seemed trapped in her beauty, desperate to ignore it, or perhaps to reveal who she was behind it.

3 When I was young I was thought a beauty – 'Beautiful Valerie Richards', they said. At one level, I had to believe it; at another, I had to struggle to rise above it.

4 Her name is Valerie Richards. She is very beautiful and very uncomfortable with it.

5 My best friend Valerie Richards is just gorgeous. Everybody – men and women too – are struck by her looks. Like struck stupid and struck by love, by which they usually mean sex. They don't have a clue what she's really like as a person. They don't want to know, do they?

6 Yes, she was beautiful. Even as I write this, I see her. Breathtaking, heartbreaking – although Valerie said this of me. Everyone saw her shyness. They couldn't see her meanness, but I can hear her countering that it was only her fright. I don't buy that, or maybe I never figured out what she was afraid of, unless it was the fear she'd be found out to be, under that beauty, not very interesting.

7 Valerie Richards, apple trees in full bloom, a jungle waterfall among a wall of orchids, your favourite Cole Porter song sung by Ella, skin soft as a Renoir, sexy as a Modigliani. Choose your own cliché – that's her.

8 There was once a princess named Valerie Richards. Her story had a curse: the more she insisted she was not a princess, the more people were convinced she was.

The following comments on each of the above statements are suggestions of possible/probable inferences of character development related to the narrative person, tense and point of view. You should try to think of at least one other possible/probable inference of character development for each.

- **Statement 1:** Standard, direct third person, past tense, generally means what it says. But the word 'generally' could indicate that the occasional or exceptional instance might be a significant part of the character's development. The seemingly objective narrative voice could turn out to be another character who knows VR and who may, therefore, not be objective at all.

- **Statement 2:** The first-person narrator, in saying 'I always felt sorry', may be indicating that she/he once knew VR but no longer does, or even that VR has died. At face value, the narrator shows sympathetic concern, but this might be a case of an unreliable narrator. Anything might have happened.
- **Statement 3:** This is VR herself as first-person narrator. 'When I was young' could indicate that she is now old and no longer 'thought a beauty' or perhaps that she lost her looks earlier in life. The tone is formal, suggesting a well-educated person. There's also a sense of high-toned moral awareness in 'to rise above it'. The story might well be driven by this struggle.
- **Statement 4:** This terse, third-person, present-tense statement keeps its cards to its chest. Its objective tone suspends judgement; the strongest hint of story mechanism is in the word 'uncomfortable'.
- **Statement 5:** The first-person voice is unlike the others. It's more colloquial, not so formally educated (the ungrammatical '*are* struck'). Does VR also regard this narrator as *her* best friend? If so, what might it say about VR's needs?
- **Statement 6:** This is the narrator as VR's disenchanted ex-lover/ partner, Did they really break each other's heart? And is the final statement true or just sour grapes? You'd certainly expect what follows to reveal at least as much of the narrator as of VR.
- **Statement 7:** The narrator's purple prose is a set-up for the cynical reversal at the end, where you, the reader, are implicated in the superficial, clichéd assessment of VR. On the other hand, saying the cliché *is* her appears to mean you'd be right in your judgement. Is the narrator sincere or is this the bitterness of rejection?
- **Statement 8:** This third-person narration uses the convention of the fairy tale. This convention makes some sense inasmuch as VR has difficulty breaking out of the (gilded) prison of her appearance. The convention has long been used, even before the 1960s, when Angela Carter and Robert Coover reworked fairy tales, notably by D.H. Lawrence in his 1926 story 'Rocking Horse Winner'.

Use a statement to write your own opening

Choose one of the eight statements above as the opening of a piece of fiction and continue it for 300–500 words more. It's useful before you begin to decide whether this is to be the opening of a novel or a short story.

The significance of the narrator

Kazio Ishiguro's 2009 story **'Crooner'** is a good illustration of the key idea above. The story is narrated by a guitarist working in Venice who recognizes a famous American pop singer and becomes involved with him and his business in Venice. This business, the ostensible story narrated, would, told by anyone else, be a grotesque satire on showbiz relationships. Only this particular narrator would take it seriously, would find a way to rationalize its inversion of values.

The opening paragraph sets out the conjunction of the narrator and Tony Gardner, the crooner. The following three paragraphs further individuate the narrator. He's not a permanent member of one of Piazza San Marco's café orchestras, but, like some others, he moves between cafés as they require a guitarist. He's not Italian, so he plays what's asked of him and doesn't make waves. The picture is built up of someone rather shy and inward-looking, of an outsider. Only then does Jan, the narrator, return to Gardner:

> *Anyway, there we were that spring morning, playing in front of a good crowd of tourists, when I saw Tony Gardner, sitting alone with his coffee, almost directly in front of us, maybe six metres back from our marquee. We get famous people in the square all the time, we never make a fuss. At the end of a number, maybe a quiet word will go around the band members. Look, there's Warren Beatty. Look, it's Kissinger. That woman, she's the one who was in the movie about the men who swap faces. We're used to it. This is the Piazza San Marco after all. But when I realized it was Tony Gardner sitting there, that was different. I did get excited. Tony Gardner had been my mother's favourite. Back home, back in the communist days, it had been really hard to get records like that, but my mother had pretty much his whole collection. Once when I was a boy, I scratched one of those precious records. The apartment was so cramped, and a boy my*

*age, you just had to move around sometimes, especially
during those cold months when you couldn't go outside.
So I was playing this game jumping from our little sofa
to the armchair, and one time I misjudged it and hit the
record player. The needle went across the record with a
zip – this was long before CDs – and my mother came in
from the kitchen and began shouting at me. I felt so bad,
not just because she was shouting at me, but because I
knew it was one of Tony Gardner's records, and I knew
how much it meant to her. And I knew that this one too
would now have those popping noises going through it
while he crooned those American songs. Years later, when
I was working in Warsaw and I got to know about black-
market records, I gave my mother replacements of all
her worn-out Tony Gardner albums, including that one I
scratched. It took me over three years, but I kept getting
them, one by one, and each time I went back to see her
I'd bring her another. So you see why I got so excited
when I recognized him, barely six metres away. At first I
couldn't quite believe it, and I might have been a beat late
with a chord change. Tony Gardner! What would my dear
mother have said if she'd known! For her sake, for the
sake of her memory, I had to go and say something to him,
never mind if the other musicians laughed and said I was
acting like a bell-boy.*

Yes, the narrator gets back to Tony Gardner, but only to say that
the local musicians were used to seeing tourist celebrities and were
quite blasé about them. So was he, except for Tony Gardner. He then
goes back to his childhood, his small apartment, and his mother and
her love for Tony Gardner records. And he recalls how, playing, he
accidentally scratched one and was made unhappy by his mother's
unhappiness at this. He tells how, older, working in Warsaw, he
manages to find, buy and replace on the black market all his
mother's Tony Gardner collection. These gifts of love and devotion
are very important to him, and when he tells you 'For her sake,
for the sake of her memory' he has to go over and say something
to Gardner, you know Gardner is a sort of icon in his mind at the
shrine of his late mother. Her love of Gardner's crooning is a father
substitute for his real father, who, significantly, is never mentioned,
the inference being that he wasn't there as Jan grew up.

By this point, you understand that the narrator has to be at least as important a character as Gardner, given the depth of background exposition of his character. And all this further substantiates Jan's passive, outsider nature. When he goes over to Gardner and explains that he's a musician in the café band, and that not only is he an admirer of Gardner's singing but that his mother had been a great fan, Gardner invites him to join him and brings the conversation back to Jan's mother. It is at this point that the 'story' of Jan and Gardner begins.

So I sat down and told him some more. About my mother, our apartment, the black-market records. And though I couldn't remember what the albums were called, I started describing the pictures on their sleeves the way I remembered them, and each time I did this, he'd put his finger up in the air and say something like: 'Oh, that would be Inimitable. The Inimitable Tony Gardner.' *I think we were both really enjoying this game, but then I noticed Mr Gardner's gaze move off me, and I turned just in time to see a woman coming up to our table.*

That 'Mr' before Gardner's name is very good. You experience Jan's respect, the good little, quiet little boy in him still, the immature awe so necessary to narrate what transpires, as if Gardner and his wife – the approaching woman – were not emotionally and morally bizarre. The story's plot proceeds from this conversation. After his wife, striking looking though older close to than she first appears, leaves the table, Gardner asks Jan to accompany him on guitar that evening when he serenades her from a gondola on a canal beneath their hotel room's balcony. Jan of course is thrilled to be musically involved with his mother's idol and naturally assumes this romantic gesture marks some special occasion for the couple. And it turns out that, indeed, the long-married Gardners spent their honeymoon in Venice, so Jan, as you do, assumes that this is a sweet rededication of their love.

It turns out, as told by Gardner in a serious tone, that this trip sadly marks the end of their marriage. Jan tells Gardner he's sorry they don't love each other any more, but Gardner corrects his naive misunderstanding to explain that the sad thing is that they really do love each other, that over the years of their marriage they have fallen deeply in love, but his career – his big comeback plan, requires a new young wife. And he's thinking of Lindy, his beloved wife, in this: he wants to leave her while she's still attractive enough to make another good marriage. Lindy, he adds, of course understands all this. Now you see how important Jan's particular character is in being able to seriously narrate this. Anyone else of normal intelligence would be aghast or find comically revealing this shallow, self-serving rationale and wouldn't be able to carry on with helping to service Gardner's grossly selfish sentimentality; that is, wouldn't be able to narrate the story.

So you read on, sort of dumbfounded, placed in a weirdly uncomfortable position by this nice narrator and his rather pathetic devotion to Gardner and the emotionally freakish world he and his wife inhabit. You might want to laugh, but then you'd be laughing at poor Jan, too. So you read on about these exotics from Planet Showbiz. And at no point does the narrator comment on the immorality of what's taking place.

> *So I played the chords in that key, and after maybe a whole verse had gone by, Mr Gardner began to sing, very softly, under his breath, like he could only half-remember the words. But his voice resonated well in that quiet canal. In fact, it sounded really beautiful. And for a moment it was like I was a boy again, back in that apartment, lying on the carpet while my mother sat on the sofa, exhausted, or maybe heartbroken, while Tony Gardner's album spun in the corner of the room.*

You can hardly laugh at the narrator's memory, yet this makes the reader at some level as implicated in the immorality of what's taking place as the narrator. And this is precisely why this limpid writing so powerfully evokes character, attracting you while repelling you.

Furthermore, and this is basic, vital to character, Jan is a musician, and he would naturally place great value on performing with someone he regards, after all, as a consummate musical artist. Gardner's musical status takes precedence over other considerations. And Jan doesn't know Americans very well. For him, they may all be a little strange.

But Ishiguro takes care to keep Jan's adulation within the bounds of belief. Towards the story's end, Jan challenges Gardner leaving his wife this way on Gardner's own terms, by pointing out that many of his greatest songs have been about people falling out of love, but many showed that 'if they go on loving each other, they should stay together for ever. That's what these songs are saying.' Gardner replies that, though it may sound hard, 'that's the way it is'. This is not much of an argument, but it's at this point that Gardner puts in his mawkishly self-serving rationale about his wife: 'She needs to get out now, while she has time. Time to find love again, make another marriage.' And then Gardner, always clever in his own defence, uses his knowledge of Jan's background to deflect all criticism. Jan responds to the comment about Lindy Gardner with: 'I don't know what I would have said to that, but then he caught me by surprise, saying: "Your mother. I guess she never got out."' To which Jan says, 'I thought about it, then said quietly, "No, Mr Gardner. She never got out. She didn't live long enough to see the changes in our country."'

Rather then understand Gardner's cynical way of changing the subject, Jan ends with the rather miserable non-sequitur about Poland. In his adulation of Gardner he assumes that 'getting out' means getting away from communism rather than getting away from loneliness into another love, into making 'another marriage'.

The depth of development in this story lies in the narrator, a person, as opposed to the ostensible subject, Gardner, merely a personality.

> ## Key idea
>
>
>
> First-person narration brings the narrator into the fiction that is being related – into its emotions and values – whether or not the narrator is conscious of it.

Narrative point of view

Narrative point of view can be problematical for some at the early stages of their writing careers. If you were using directly autobiographical incidents and yourself as the central character, you might have found yourself getting too close to what you wrote. 'Too close' in this sense means being so involved in recreating your own past that you couldn't see where the *character* might not be clearly written, or where the character might go on so long and so obviously about what was taking place that readers would have lost interest, or where events that still fascinated you were of too little significance to the story's development to be included. Another way of putting this is that relatively unpractised writers have to learn to differentiate between what might personally satisfy them as autobiography and what is needed to satisfy readers as an experience of fiction. Writers have to be able to see the insect on the bark of a tree as well as the shape of the woods the tree helps form.

Sometimes it's helpful to put the character back into the context of the story by changing the narrative viewpoint. This might mean shifting from first-person to third-person narration, or from narration by the main character to narration by a less central character. Sometimes, after rewriting a few scenes this way, the writer gains enough 'distance' – by which is meant enough critical perspective on that character – to write the story or novel (or part of it, if there are to be multiple narrators) back in the original first-person point of view.

You, however, as a more advanced writer, will have worked this out through trial and error, the rewrites and edits of your writing practice. At the least, you'll try to be aware of the implications of your choices in narration.

Write an 'unconscious' narrator

Write a 750–1,000-word opening of a piece of fiction in first-person narration in which the narrator introduces the story of someone else with a moral dilemma/shortcoming/fall without being aware of her/his own collusion.

FIRST-PERSON NARRATION

Going back to Chapter 2's discussion of Claire Messud's *The Woman Upstairs*, you'll recall the intensity of its first-person opening: the rage about being 'invisible' rather than 'flying', the feeling of betrayal – by others and herself – and the dedication to 'make my nothingness count'. The novel goes on to tell the story about Nora, the narrator, being taken up by a family, the child in Nora's class, his mother a well-known installation artist, and the father a visiting academic specializing in the ethics of history. This family has come over from Paris for one year when the father has a fellowship at Harvard. Nora tells how she comes to fall in love with the entire glamorous, sensitive family, how she comes first to babysit for the son Reza and then how she shares a studio with the mother, Sirena. With these people, especially Sirena, Nora comes to feel that for the first time in her life she is deeply understood, *recognized* for the artist she knows she is at the core of her being. The novel goes on to tell how these people, Sirena (the 'siren') especially, come to betray all the deepest confidences that Nora has opened up to let them see who she really is within the exterior of good daughter, good teacher, good friend, and really nice (merely nice) person.

First-person narration seems a natural enough choice for a novel in which the central character reveals how she finally reveals herself to people she trusts, people, especially the artist Sirena, who recognize in Nora a fellow artist, who encourage, praise and urge on this inner person who is invisible, really, to the rest of the world.

And what is Nora's art? She makes little rooms, really little replicas of the rooms of 'outsider' women artists with whom she identifies – Emily Dickinson, Virginia Woolf, Alice Neel and Edie Sedgewick. These rooms, or the ones she almost finishes during the novel's timeframe, are made with great attention to detail, with painstaking craft. But they are so small that they can only be viewed by one person at a time. Little rooms, like doll's house rooms. Sirena, on the other hand, is working in her half of the studio on an enormous installation of Wonderland, in which lots and lots of people can be Alice at any one time. As opposed to Nora, Sirena is making something to be experienced by a large audience, she's making something to be seen and to interact with rather than to peek into, one eye at one tiny window at a time. Swept up into Sirena's world, Nora actually helps Sirena turn some of her concepts into material elements of the installation. Since she feels fully alive for the first time, she finds she has energy for everything – her father, her friends, her teaching, her own art and Sirena's art, too. She is now visible, not merely a succession of pleasant masks. Certainly, first-person narration is the most intimate way of presenting this inner awakening.

And yet the irony, the novel's high irony, is that Nora is not a real artist. High craft, yes, the craft, perhaps of an artist, but not the temperament it takes to be an artist, since Nora will never show what she makes to anyone but those she knows and loves and trusts. Skandar, Sirena's husband, hints at this when she shows him her little 'room' and he wonders out loud why her work is so tiny, the implication in context being why is it so exclusive, so excluding of any real audience?

The novel's ending circles back to its opening. Sirena, the real artist, has so used Nora, so abused Nora, that she vows she's now going to use her rage and anger (with which the book opened) to really 'live', to really, you think, become that artist, a real artist.

But then you doubt it. Ibsen's Nora actually walks out of the stultifying home at the end of *A Doll's House*; Messud's Nora is still inside, only promising to leave. This is a brilliant use of first-person narration, deeply revealing, deeply self-deceiving.

Write a self-contradiction

Write a 250-word, first-person narration of the opening of a piece of fiction in which the reader can see something isn't quite right, is a self-contradiction – yet which makes the reader want to read on.

THIRD-PERSON OMNISCIENCE

Doris Lessing's well-known short story **'To Room Nineteen'** (1978) is also about what you could call the 'doll's house syndrome', the woman's growing alienation from her conventional woman's life. But this is narrated in almost strict omniscient third person. Almost, except for its opening sentence: 'This is a story, I suppose, about a failure in intelligence: the Rawlings' marriage was grounded in intelligence.' The narrator never again steps forward into the first person.

Just what is meant by 'a failure in intelligence' you find out by reading the story. The next paragraph sets the narrative tone.

> *They were older when they married than most of their married friends: in their well-seasoned late twenties. Both had had a number of affairs, sweet rather than bitter; and when they fell in love – for they did fall in love – had known each other for some time. They joked that they had saved each other 'for the real thing'. That they had waited so long (but not too long) for this real thing was to them a proof of their sensible discrimination. A good many of their friends had married young, and now (they felt) probably regretted lost opportunities; while others, still unmarried, seemed to them arid, self-doubting, and likely to make desperate or romantic marriages.*

The sting is at the tail of the paragraph, where 'romantic marriages' are deemed by the Rawlings to be a mistake. Yet they themselves 'did fall in love'. What you can make of that is their idea that 'well-seasoned' love is 'sensible'; romantic marriages involve something shallower. Do they put too much confidence in the 'well-seasoned' or too little in the 'romantic'? Is neither of them in any way 'romantic'? You note in all this how clear and distinct the third-person omniscient narration is. One advantage of third-person omniscience is its ability to control pace; to move from slow detailed description to fast summary, as in the following paragraph:

*And this is what happened. They lived in their charming
flat for two years, giving parties and going to them, being
a popular young married couple, and then Susan became
pregnant, she gave up her job, and they bought a house
in Richmond. It was typical of this couple that they had
a son first, then a daughter, then twins, son and daughter.
Everything right, appropriate, and what everyone would
wish for, if they could choose. But people did feel these two
had chosen; this balanced and sensible family was no more
than what was due to them because of their infallible sense
for choosing right.*

Very fast, very direct, yet very strange, this insistence on meeting
certain standards. Never the question why right? or why
appropriate? or why would everyone wish for this? Who was
'everyone'? The omniscient narrator chose 'right' rather than 'good',
'appropriate' rather than 'happy'. Just as revealing is that the
narrator does not say that this was a loving family, does not speak
of Sally's and Matthew's feelings. It's very much description from
the outside; you're put in the position of those people who knew
them, who felt them 'balanced and sensible' and that they 'invariably
made the right choices'. But right for *what*? Everything seems to
go without saying, certainly without reference to feelings or to any
sense of *meaning*.

The paragraphs that follow this begin to bring some shadow into
the sunlit lives of this picture-perfect couple.

*And so they lived with their four children in their gardened
house in Richmond and were happy. They had everything
that they had wanted and had planned for.*

And yet...

*Well, even this was expected, that there must
be a certain flatness...*

*Yes, yes, of course, it was natural they sometimes felt like
this. Like what?*

*Their life seemed to be like a snake biting its tail.
Matthew's job for the sake of Susan, children, house, and
garden – which caravanserai needed a well-paid job to
maintain it. And Susan's practical intelligence for the sake*

of Matthew, the children, the house and the garden – which unit would have collapsed in a week without her.

But there was no point about which either could say: 'For the sake of this is all the rest.' Children? But children can't be the centre of a life and a reason for being. They can be a thousand things that are delightful, interesting, satisfying, but they can't be a wellspring to live from. Or they shouldn't be. Susan and Matthew knew that well enough. Matthew's job? Ridiculous. It was an interesting job, but scarcely a reason for living. Matthew took pride in doing it well, but he could hardly be expected to be proud of the newspaper; the newspaper he read, his newspaper, was not the one he worked for.

Their love for each other? Well, that was the nearest it. If this wasn't a centre, what was? Yes, it was around this point, their love, that the whole of the extraordinary structure revolved. For extraordinary it certainly was. Both Susan and Matthew had moments of thinking so, of looking in secret disbelief at this thing they had created: marriage, four children, big house, garden, charwomen, friends, cars... and this thing, this entity, all of it had come into existence, been blown into being out of nowhere, because Susan loved Matthew and Matthew loved Susan. Extraordinary. So that was the central point, the wellspring.

And if one felt that it simply was not strong enough, important enough, to support it all, well whose fault was that? Certainly neither Susan's nor Matthew's. It was in the nature of things. And they sensibly blamed neither themselves nor each other.

On the contrary, they used their intelligence to preserve what they had created from a painful and explosive world: they looked around them, and took lessons. All around them, marriages collapsing, or breaking, or rubbing along (even worse, they felt).

They must not make the same mistakes, they must not.

What happens from '*And yet...*' is an argument. It isn't dialogue, isn't literally between Susan and Matthew, nor is it the sort of nineteenth-century omniscient narrator who dictates to you what a character should or should not be doing or thinking or feeling. This narration takes who the characters are – the intelligent, up-to-date, well-read, sophisticated couple – and argues 'and yet' from their own belief systems. So Matthew's job isn't 'it'. Nor is Susan's home management. And even the children – delightful, fascinating as they are – 'can't' be it, or 'shouldn't be'. What's left: their love for each other. Oh. Yes, by a process of elimination, 'their' argument (the narration's version of it) you find, is that it's love, love, love, the reason for and 'wellspring' of life. This long, rather tortuous argument with its near surprise conclusion, this 'extraordinary' reason for everything should make you, the reader, at least slightly uncomfortable, as if ordinary, basic feeling has to be forced from these two who have so over intellectualized themselves, whose intellectual vanities have so insulated and isolated them from messy, violent, chaotic reality. Theirs is a dangerous rigidity of spirit, especially as it includes an assumed 'understanding' of all that 'reality'. Nonetheless, there is love.

This section ends with Susan and Matthew satisfied that their high 'intelligence' will enable them to learn from a world of failed marriages – especially those where the couple remained together after love was gone, the worst kind – how to sustain their own. And since both of them were aware of the possible resentments of the woman who'd given up her career for marriage and motherhood, they each intelligently spoke of their day – he at work, she at home – lying in their 'big married bed in the big married bedroom', and so avoided the problems of couples who don't tell each other of their day. Yet the doubling of 'big married' is ominous, the narrator suggesting something amiss, an over-dependency on the setting, the trappings, rather than the feelings. Again, you note how the narration insinuates and assumes characters' attitudes.

Key idea

Third-person narration can successfully shift from relative objectivity into a subjective point of view identical to that of the characters.

A few paragraphs later, you come to 'So what did it matter if they felt dry, flat? People like themselves, fed on a hundred books (psychological, anthropological, sociological), could scarcely be unprepared for the dry, controlled wistfulness which is the distinguishing mark of the intelligent marriage.' The emotional repression is frightening. You read this and, if it hasn't struck you before, you're now aware of that 'failure of intelligence' suggested in the story's opening sentence.

So love is the mainspring, but then you read: 'this was life, that two people, no matter how carefully chosen, could not be everything to each other. In fact, even to say so, to think in such a way, was banal; they were ashamed to do it.' Ashamed, you think, to acknowledge the real sadness of it even to themselves, caught in the intellectual conceit that they, of all people, were self-sufficient, didn't need the help of others. The next paragraph continues:

> *It was banal, too, when one night Matthew came home late and confessed he had been to a party, taken a girl home and slept with her. Susan forgave him, of course. Except that forgiveness is hardly the word. Understanding, yes. But if you understand something you don't forgive it, you are the thing itself: forgiveness is for what you* don't *understand. Nor had he confessed – what sort of word is that?*

The narration here brilliantly creates the doublethink, the nonsensical 'intelligence' with which Susan's emotions are cornered and caged. The first two sentences get it right; Matthew did 'confess', Susan did 'forgive'. But the rigid self-image of their intelligent superiority overcomes her genuine feelings, and the rest of the paragraph is Susan's intellectual rebuttal of her initial emotional honesty. She 'intelligently' convinces herself that there was nothing to confess, nothing to forgive (and that Matthew's selfish 'sharing' of this event with her was itself, therefore, nothing).

This, coming on the fourth page of a story that is more than 28 pages long, is actually the climax, the emotional turning point. Of course, these two people can't, won't, recognize it. But from this point on, everything has less and less meaning to Susan – the children, the lovely house and garden on the river at Richmond, darling Matthew himself. 'After all, years ago they had joked: Of course I'm not going to be faithful to you, no one can be faithful to one other person for a whole lifetime. (And there was the word "faithful" – stupid, all these words, stupid, belonging to a savage old world.)' Here the third-person narration becomes heartbreaking in its coldly logical perversity.

Susan therefore knows the 'sensible' thing to do is to put this meaningless, banal one-night sex of Matthew with someone else behind her. It had made her cry, stupidly, and Matthew had eased her then by making passionate love to her. Generous Matthew, you think ironically, fucking two women in the same night. From this time on, Susan's lovely home and garden give her headaches, even the lovely children 'somehow' give her headaches. She longs to be just herself, alone with herself, not so hemmed in by these others.

First she leaves the house and sits in the garden, but she can hear the housekeeper from there. Her youngest children, the twins, go off to school, but the freedom everyone told her this would bring for her never materializes. Freedom to do what? To be what? So she fixes up the spare room at the top of the house to be her very own private space. But once there, alone, 'she felt even more caged there than in her bedroom'. She finds herself mending the children's clothes in this room.

Susan then gets the idea that someone awful, like the devil she knew didn't exist, was lurking in the garden, 'and he wants to *get into me and to take me over...*' If only, she thinks, she could have a place away from all this, a room of one's own, a room in which she could be herself. So she takes a room in a genteel hotel in London, but, somehow, the genteel woman running the hotel looks to her for companionship when she brings Susan tea, and so somehow ruins any chance of her truly being herself on her own. Then she finds an unlikely place for someone like herself, a seedy hotel in Paddington. By now she also employs a German au pair who completely takes over looking after the children. As all this happens, Matthew is totally understanding. In her room at the wonderfully named 'Fred's Hotel' ('The façade was a faded shiny yellow, like unhealthy skin'), she does nothing but sit in an armchair and fall asleep. Or she sits in the armchair and goes to the window and looks down, 'loving the men and women who passed, because she did not know them'. She looks at the sky, at the buildings, and returns to the chair, her mind empty. She 'brooded, wondered, simply went dark, feeling emptiness run deliciously through her veins like the movement of her blood'. You know she's in real trouble.

This anonymous room totally suits her. Matthew, of course, gives her the money to rent it during the weekdays. Unquestioningly.

Things get worse: Matthew asks if she wants a divorce, so she intelligently reasons that he must assume she's seeing a lover in the hotel. Worse, more cleverly, she reasons that Matthew hopes she has a lover, since believing she went there to merely sit and do nothing and think of nothing would for him be much more frightening. Suspicious, at the hotel she asks Fred if anyone has been around asking questions about her. He eventually admits that someone has been around, but all he's said is that Mrs Jones (her alias) comes 'every weekday from ten until five or six and stayed in Number 19 by herself'. She knows this man must be a detective hired by

Matthew. This must mean he knows she doesn't have a lover, knows there must be something wrong with her. This means there's no use for the room any more because it's now spoiled, part of the world where she's not truly on her own, not herself.

When she tells Matthew she no longer needs the money to rent the room, they talk about it and he admits he's been worried and hired someone to find out about it, because he has been worried, wondering… Rather than tell him the truth, she finishes his idea with, 'You thought I had a lover?'

She cannot bring herself to say she's been sitting in a sordid hotel room doing nothing for five days a week and being quite content. Instead, she continues with what she understands to be the less awful justification for the room: 'Well, perhaps you're not far wrong.' At this, Matthew says with relief, 'In that case I must confess I've got a bit of an affair on myself.' Stunned, she pretends interest, asks who the woman is, and he, of course, tells her – someone they both knew in their unmarried days. Eventually, Matthew suggests the 'civilized' thing, that they make it a foursome. They could all meet for lunch. Again caught in her own pretence, she says, 'Why not?' He says, 'I mean, it's ridiculous, you sneaking off to filthy hotels, and me staying late at the office and all the lies everyone has to tell.' In a panic, Susan makes up the name 'Michael' for her lover, saying he's away at the moment. But 'Inside she was dissolving in horror at them both, at how far they had both sunk from honesty of emotion.'

Something has at last registered in Susan, but far too late. Emotional honesty has been consistently sacrificed to clever, fashionable, deceiving intelligence, to the social conformity of 'playing the game', in which playing turns out to be no substitute for living. Now, somehow, she's promised that her invented lover Michael Plant will turn up in a few days for a 'jolly' foursome at lunch. She even, for a moment, considers hiring someone to play the role of 'Michael', but she finds this too grotesque. She can't any longer go on with the farce. Nor, of course, can she admit to Matthew that he's broken her heart. That she loved him and his faithlessness has destroyed her, and that this began way back with his little one-night affair.

Susan returns to Fred's Hotel and once more rents Room 19. This time, she sees the obvious traces of the couple who've just left it. She stands at the window again, watching the people pass. She tries to think of what she must first do, but it simply tires her. She sinks into a dark, delightful daydream in which she's sliding to the edge of a river. Then she gets up, pushes the rug against the door, checks that the window is shut, puts two shillings in the meter and turns on the gas. Finally she lies on the bed, 'that smelled stale, that smelled of sweat and sex'. Her legs feel chilly so she covers them with a blanket and lies back 'quite content, listening to the faint soft hiss of the gas that poured into the room, into her lungs, into her brain, as she drifted off into the dark river'.

This 85 per cent of the story is one of the longest denouements you'll ever read, but the narration justifies it, constantly placing you where the character herself hardly dares to go – inside herself to her feelings. That she can't find anything there doesn't, of course, mean that you can't. You see that so rigidly does she cling to the illusions of her intelligence and good sense that she would rather see herself as empty inside than as hurt, rejected, confused, and yearning for love. For her, the only way to confront this comforting nothingness is to go into it permanently and end her life.

Not only is third-person omniscient narration the logical choice, it is the only one which can enliven the writing with its constant commentaries, interior dialogues consciously rejected, and its few but vital gaps through which the truth slips out.

Unlike Claire Messud's Nora, who vows at the end of the novel to break out of her self-designed doll's house into becoming a real artist, but whom you don't, on the whole, believe can do it, Lessing's Susan seems to leap from her gilded cage before your eyes, with a terrible, calm determination. As the opening sentence said, 'a failure in intelligence'. And yet you may recall that that same sentence is when the narrator for once reveals herself in the first person, saying only 'I suppose'.

Second-person narration

It's possible, of course, to narrate in the second person. For example:

> *You wake late in the morning. You go out to the store on the corner for bread and milk. Bill is behind the counter as usual, but when you say 'Morning, Bill', he says he's not Bill, and when you ask where Bill is, he says there's no one working here called Bill. His name is Rudolph, he says, and it's his shop. You nod, afraid to ask if he recognizes you.*

This point of view is not much used, especially in longer short stories and novels. It may be that writers find the artifice of constantly invoking the reader to become the character too stilted to maintain. And if 'you' is supposed to mean 'anyone', writers may find it more comfortable to write in the third person: 'She wakes late... He wakes late.'

Its main use is to shift out of the third or first person into a tone more immediately informal. Hemingway used it, as here in *The Sun Also Rises* (*Fiesta*), to break from the first person and then return to it:

> *The nights were cold and the days were hot, and there was always a breeze even in the heat of the day. It was hot enough so that it felt good to wade in a cold stream, and the sun dried you when you came out and sat on the bank. We found a stream with a pool deep enough to swim in.*

Workshop

Consider the following in relation to your own fiction:

- Is most or all of your fiction narrated in the same person? Is that third person or first person?
- If the answer to the above question is 'yes', why do you think that is? If you answer that you're more comfortable in that person of narration, what in detail do you mean by 'comfortable?'
- How much thought do you give before starting a first draft to the idea of narrative point of view?
- Do you vary narrative viewpoint from one work of fiction to another? What are some deciding factors for you?
- Do you consider narrative point of view important to the tone of your writing?
- Do you feel that you have developed your own fictional voice? If so, how important is narrative point of view to your voice?
- Would it cease to be your voice if you wrote from a narrative viewpoint you never or rarely use?
- Ask yourself the above two points with regard to tense of presentation.

Try to apply the above questions and ideas to specific pieces of your writing rather than thinking of them as somehow 'theoretical' questions.

Focus points

- Some fiction requires a special sort of narrator, someone with very particular characteristics, in order to be 'told'.
- Among the demands made of narration is the ability to depict character interiority. 'Interiority' means not only a character's inner thoughts and feelings but also the experience of the reader that unconscious emotions and ideas are being evoked.
- It is possible to use first-, third- and even second-person narration and shift between them.

Next step

The next chapter begins a two-chapter study of showing *character. The first of these chapters looks at action and character development.*

5

Showing character through action

Current critical opinion in fiction generally has it as better to show than to tell. This certainly extends to character. 'Don't tell the reader about your character, show the reader your character' is an often expressed critique in fiction workshops and masterclasses. However, this instruction can become obsessive and unhelpful, because there remains the need in much fiction for the narrator to tell the reader about setting, situational background and, yes, the characters.

Nevertheless, showing character in action is a direct and imaginatively stimulating method of engaging the reader in the shared process – the creative reading – of fiction. In this sense, 'action' means the character's physical actions *including* dialogue. Since this is so large a topic, discussion of physical action and dialogue each merit a whole chapter. This chapter focuses on the description of characters' physical actions: what it consists of and how it develops character.

Slow action

A short story well known for the dominance of physical action is Jack London's **'To Build a Fire'**, published in 1908. In it, the single human character is unnamed. He's a man new to the arctic winter of the Yukon, and he and his husky dog are walking a small trail to get to a mining camp and warmth. There's no direct sunlight in the daytime yet, even though it's almost the start of spring. He's properly dressed for the trek, to the standards of those days, though he judges the temperature at the outset to be 'fifty degrees below zero'. But once he sets out, he finds it's even colder: '…he spat speculatively. There was a sharp, explosive crackle that startled him. He spat again. And again, in the air, before it could fall to the snow, the spittle crackled. He knew that at fifty below spittle crackled on the snow, but this spittle crackled in the air.'

So he knows it's extremely cold. He also knows that since the trail is essentially over frozen creeks, he'll have to take great care not to break through the occasional springs that never freeze, invisible under the snow. If he did, he'd have to build a fire and dry his feet and socks and moccasins to keep his feet from freezing.

He takes care, but it happens – he falls through into spring water and wets himself up to his calves. He's angry at himself because this means it will take him an extra hour to get to the camp. There follows a description in meticulous detail of him locating a deposit of dry sticks and twigs up on the bank beneath the trees. As he builds the fire, he thinks:

> *…there must be no failure. When it is seventy-five below zero, a man must not fail in his first attempt to build a fire – that is, if his feet are wet. If his feet are dry, and he fails, he can run along the trail for half a mile and restore his circulation. But the circulation of wet and freezing feet cannot be restored by running when it is seventy-five below. No matter how fast he runs, the wet feet will freeze the harder.*

As his fire is beginning to burn well, he remembers an old-timer's advice that, after fifty below, no man should travel alone in the Klondike. But he's young and strong and thinks the old man was something of a fearful old maid. Any real man can do it. But 'he had not thought his fingers could go lifeless in so short a time. Lifeless they were, for he could scarcely make them move together to grip a twig, and they seemed remote from his body and from him. When he touched a twig, he had to look and see whether or not he had hold of it!'

He starts untying his moccasins to dry them, but realizing his fingers are too numb to cope with knots, he draws his knife to cut them.

But before he could cut the strings, it happened. It was his own fault or, rather, his mistake. He should not have built the fire under the spruce tree. He should have built it in the open. But it had been easier to pull the twigs from the brush and drop them directly on to the fire. Now the tree under which he had done this carried a weight of snow on its boughs. No wind had blown for weeks, and each bough was fully freighted. Each time he had pulled a twig he had communicated a slight agitation to the tree – an imperceptible agitation, so far as he was concerned, but an agitation sufficient to bring about the disaster. High up in the tree one bough capsized its load of snow. This fell on the boughs below, capsizing them. This process continued, spreading and involving the whole tree. It grew like an avalanche, and it descended without warning upon the man and the fire, and the fire was blotted out!

The following summary is necessary to the points to be made on this particular method of presenting action.

Temporarily stunned, the man knows he must build his fire again, this time without failure. If he succeeds, as things stand, he understands he's likely to lose some toes to frostbite. So once again he sets to work, and once again London describes with the same focus on detail the man collecting and moving from under the tree the twigs and branches. But now, his numb fingers aren't able to separate out the wet moss and twigs. When all is ready to start the fire, he reaches into his pocket for the dry birch bark he uses as tinder. He can hear it crinkle but he can't grasp it with his fingers so numb. He pulls his mittens back on with his teeth and begins beating his hands against his sides until he feels, with great pain, the sensation returning with circulation to his hands. He then takes off his right mitten and gets out the birch bark and then his bunched sulphur matches. In trying to separate off one match from the bunch, his fingers, grown numb once more, drop the matches into the snow.

'He drove the thought of his freezing feet, and nose, and cheeks, out of his mind, devoting his whole soul to the matches. He watched, using the sense of vision in place of that of touch, and when he saw his fingers on each side of the bunch, he closed them – that is, he willed to close them, for the wires were down and the fingers did not obey.'

Once again, he pulls on the mitten and beats his right hand 'fiercely against his knee'. Finally, he gets the matches, 'with much snow, into his lap'. He manages, using the heels of both hands, to get the bunch of matches to his mouth.

The ice crackled and snapped when by a violent effort he opened his mouth. He drew the lower jaw in, curled the upper lip out of the way, and scraped the bunch with his upper teeth in order to separate a match. He succeeded in getting one, which he dropped on his lap. He was no better off. He could not pick it up. Then he devised a way. He picked it up in his teeth and scratched it on his leg. Twenty times he scratched before he succeeded in lighting it. As it flamed he held it with his teeth to the birch bark. But the burning brimstone went up his nostrils and into his lungs, causing him to cough spasmodically. The match fell on to the snow and went out.

The old-timer on Sulphur Creek was right, he thought in the moment of controlled despair that ensued: after fifty below, a man should travel with a partner. He beat his hands, but failed in exciting any sensation. Suddenly he bared both hands, removing his mittens with his teeth. He caught the whole bunch between the heels of his hands. His arm muscles not being frozen enabled him to press the hand-heels tightly against the matches. Then he scratched the bunch along his leg. It flared into flame, seventy sulphur matches at once! There was no wind to blow them out. He kept his head to one side to escape the strangling fumes, and held the blazing bunch to the birch bark. As he so held it, he became aware of sensation in his hand. His flesh was burning. He could smell it. Deep down below the surface he could feel it. The sensation developed into pain that grew acute. And still he endured it, holding the flame of the matches clumsily to the bark that would not light readily because his own burning hands were in the way, absorbing most of the flames.

At last, when he could endure no more, he jerked his hands apart. The blazing matches fell sizzling into the snow, but the birch bark was alight. He began laying dry grasses and the tiniest twigs on the flame...

And on goes the action, at this same close focus of detailed description. And, although the man has been foolish and arrogant to land himself in this position, you have to hope he succeeds in making the fire that is his only chance of staying alive. It's not only that you are forced to identify with the human, rather than with the dog, snug in its fur; it's that you've followed the man in all his painstaking, pain-making action.

This action can be thought of as slow just because it is so fine-scaled and detailed. The large, quick actions – the man breaking through the ice, the snow falling in a sudden avalanche to put out the first fire – are the shifts in speed that in a way force the action back to its slow, that is, highly detailed and small-scale, movement.

The effect is also cumulative: the further on you read, the more significant each action becomes in determining the life-or-death outcome of the struggle between nature and human nature. The tension grows because the writer has made clear, through the man's thoughts, the continual narrowing of options left him.

 ## Write a slow-action scene

Write a 250-word opening of a scene of slow action. This means fine focus and detail. It could be anything from washing very old, rare china plates to devising a specific software program, but it must develop the character.

Fast action

At the other extreme of the pace at which action can be described and developed is the breakneck style of James Ellroy's writing in the prologue to his novel **L.A. Confidential** (1990).

An abandoned auto court in the San Berdoo foothills;
Buzz Meeks checked in with ninety-four thousand dollars,
eighteen pounds of high-grade heroin, a 10-guage pump, a
.38 special, a .45 automatic and a switchblade he'd bought
off a pachuco at the border – right before he spotted the car
parked across the line: Mickey Cohen goons in an LAPD
unmarked, Tijuana cops standing by to bootjack a piece of
his goodies, dump his body in the San Ysidro River.

After this breathless, one-sentence opening paragraph, the next
paragraph sprints through the background of how Buzz Meeks came
to be here with his particular baggage. Then it comes back to the
present scene.

Meeks ditched his car in a pine grove, hauled his suitcase
out, scoped the setup:

The motel was horseshoe-shaped, a dozen rooms, foothills
against the back of them – no rear approach possible.

The courtyard was loose gravel covered with twigs, paper
debris, empty wine bottles – footsteps would crunch, tires
would crack wood and glass.

There was only one access – the road he drove in
on – reconnoiterers would have to trek thick timber to
take a potshot.

Or they could be waiting in one of the rooms.

Meeks grabbed the 10-gauge, started kicking in doors. One,
two, three, four – cobwebs, rats, bathrooms with plugged-
up toilets, rotted food, magazines in Spanish – the runners
probably used the place to house their spics en route to the
slave farms up in Kern County. Five, six, seven. Bingo on
that – Mex families huddled on mattresses, scared of a white
man with a gun, 'There, there' to keep them pacified. The last
string of rooms stood empty; Meeks got his satchel, plopped it
down just inside unit 12; front/courtyard view, a mattress on
box springs spilling kapok, not bad for a last American flop.

Then comes a shortish paragraph as Meeks looks at a cheesecake
calendar, looks for his birthday, starts wondering whether he'll
survive the year, and becomes frightened.

*It got worse – the heebie-jeebies. Meeks laid his arsenal
on a window ledge, stuffed his pockets with ammo:
shells for the .38, spare clips for the automatic. He
tucked the switchblade into his belt, covered the back
window with the mattress, cracked the front window for
air. A breeze cooled his sweat; he looked out at spic kids
chucking a baseball.*

*He stuck there. Wetbacks congregated outside: pointing at
the sun like they were telling time by it, hot for the truck
to arrive – stoop labor for three hots and a cot. Dusk came
on; the beaners started jabbering. Meeks saw two white
men – one fat, one skinny – walk into the courtyard. They
waved glad-hander style; the spics waved back. They didn't
look like cops or Cohen goons. Meeks stepped outside, his
10-gauge right behind him.*

*The men waved: big smiles, no harm meant. Meeks
checked the road – a green sedan parked crossways,
blocking something light blue, too shiny to be sky through
fir trees, He caught light off a metallic paint job, snapped:
Bakersfield, the meet with the guys who needed time to get
the money, The robin's-egg coupe that tried to broadside
him a minute later.*

*Meeks smiled: friendly guy, no harm meant. A finger on
the trigger; a make on the skinny guy: Mal Lunceford,
a Hollywood Station harness bull – he used to ogle the
carhops at Scrivener's Drive-in, puff out his chest to show
off his pistol medals. The fat man, closer, said, 'We got that
airplane waiting.'*

*Meeks swung the shotgun around, triggered a spread.
Fat Man caught buckshot and flew, covering Lunceford –
knocking him backward. The wetbacks tore helter-skelter;
Meeks ran into the room, heard the back window breaking,
yanked the mattress. Sitting ducks, two men, three triple-
aught rounds close in.*

*The two blew up; glass and blood covered three more men
inching along the wall. Meeks leaped, hit the ground, fired
at three sets of legs pressed together; his free hand flailed,
caught a revolver off a dead man's waistband.*

Shrieks from the courtyard; running feet on gravel. Meeks dropped the shotgun, stumbled to the wall. Over to the men, tasting blood – point-blank head shots.

Thumps in the room; two rifles in grabbing range. Meeks yelled. 'We got him!', heard answering whoops, saw arms and legs coming out the window. He picked up the closest piece and let fly, full automatic: trapped targets, plaster chips exploding, dry wood igniting.

Over the bodies, into the room. The front door stood open; his pistols were still on the ledge. A strange thump sounded; Meeks saw a man spread prone – aiming from behind the mattress box.

Hew threw himself to the floor, kicked, missed. The man got off a shot – close; Meeks grabbed his switchblade, leaped, stabbed: the neck, the face, the man screaming, shooting – wide ricochets. Meeks slit his throat, crawled over and toed the door shut, grabbed the pistols and just plain breathed.

The fire spreading: cooking up bodies, fir pines; the front door the only way out. How many more men standing trigger?

Shots.

From the courtyard: heavy rounds knocking out wall chunks. Meeks caught one in the leg; a shot grazed his back. He hit the floor, the shots kept coming, the door went down – he was smack in the crossfire.

No more shots.

Meeks tucked his guns under his chest, spread himself dead-man style. Seconds dragged; four men walked in holding rifles. Whispers: 'Dead meat' – 'Let's be reeel careful' – 'Crazy Okie fuck.' Through the doorway, Mal Lunceford not one of them, footsteps.

Kicks in his side, hard breathing, sneers. A foot went under him. A voice said, 'Fat fucker.'

Meeks jerked the foot; the foot man tripped backward. Meeks spun around shooting – close range, all hits. Four men went down; Meeks got a topsy-turvy view: the

courtyard, Mal Lunceford turning tail. Then, behind him,
'Hello, lad.'

Dudley Smith stepped through flames, dressed in a fire
department greatcoat. Meeks saw his suitcase – ninety-four
grand, dope – over by the mattress. 'Dud, you came prepared.'

'Like the Boy Scouts, lad. And have you a valediction?'

Suicide: heisting a deal Dudley S. watchdogged. Meeks
raised his guns; Smith shot first. Meeks died – thinking the
El Serrano Motel looked just like the Alamo.

To write this fast, Ellroy creates an amalgam English. Its basis is
what was in the days of telegrams called telegram style. Words not
absolutely necessary are omitted, such as identifying narrative to
dialogue. So you get 'There, there, to keep them pacified', wthout
the 'Meeks said'. Commas replace conjunctions: 'The courtyard was
loose gravel covered with twigs, paper debris, empty wine bottles –'.
Pronouns and verbs are knocked out in the rush of action: 'It got
worse – the heebie-jeebies.' No 'he got'.

A second major element of this language is the journalese of the
1950s setting of the prologue, and of two particular journalistic
genres. One is the Hollywood/Broadway show-business press, such
as *Variety*, with its showbiz jargon and overstatement. The other
is the gossip magazines of the period and locale, represented in the
novel by one called *Hush Hush*, an allusion to the real magazine
Confidential. Such magazines had a low and breathless style, as if
they were whispering secrets in your ear.

And then there's Ellroy's diction, laced with local LA slang and
nickname, such as 'San Berdoo' for San Bernardino. Central to the
novel's plot and its characters is the cops-and-robbers jargon and
its racism. So Mexicans are Mex, wetbacks, spic, beaners. Meeks
'scopes' the setup. Police are 'LAPD', 'cops', 'bull', and 'make' is for
'identify'. Robbing is 'heisting' and guarded is 'watchdogged'. The
Mexicans have been taken across the US border by 'runners' and are
waiting to be picked up by trucks that will take them to 'slave farms'
where they'll work with short hoes as 'stoop labor' and earn only
bed and board, 'three hots and a cot'.

Since you don't yet know who the characters are, it's the language
and action that hold your interest. But you see that Meeks knows
that some of the characters are out to get him for the money and
drugs he's carrying. You may surmise that Meeks himself is, or was,
a Los Angeles policeman; what you're fairly sure of is that the last

man standing (Meeks himself has killed, at my count, 13 men in this prologue), Dudley Smith, will appear in the novel that follows.

In fact, the novel's plot involves the working out of events years later that stem from this bloody prologue. The prologue's job is to leave you curious to know more, to be carried into the novel by the power of its racy, racing language.

Edit exercise

Taking the same character you used in the slow-action Write exercise, develop her/him in a 250-word opening of a fast-action scene.

Key idea

Action can be presented through a range of tempos, from slow and methodically detailed to very fast and selectively elliptical. The writer's choice of the action's pace is significant to the development of character.

The London and Ellroy extracts are 'life and death' examples, but much if not most action in fiction is more everyday – yet essential to development of character. Don't be put off if you happen to know that Jack London actually took part in the Klondike (Yukon) gold rush, the setting for 'To Build a Fire'. Ellroy's materials also have autobiographical roots in that he spent years trying to understand and solve his mother's rape and murder in 1958, when he was ten years old. (You can read his moving essay on this in the Afterword to his novel *The Black Dahlia*.)

Key idea

Most people spend a great deal of their lives working and yet fiction, especially contemporary literary fiction, doesn't on the whole reflect this. It can be of critical significance to the development of character, especially in writing that purports to be within the genre of realism.

Work as action: housework

In Jane Smiley's 2004 novel *A Thousand Acres,* its narrator and protagonist Ginny is a farmer's wife in the rural Midwest and the oldest of three daughters of the county's most successful farmer. She is, like the neighbouring wives, very hardworking but, in her case, the intensity of her work is psychologically a way to keep the lid on her emotions, particularly a way to keep suppressed the great trauma of her childhood.

The novel's plot is loosely based on that of Shakespeare's *King Lear.* Ginny's father has, like Lear, decided to divide his land between his three daughters and, like Shakespeare's Cordelia, the youngest refuses to take part. In the latter part of the novel, Ginny's father, supported by his youngest daughter, takes out a lawsuit to reclaim his land from Ginny and her sister Rose. Ginny and Rose's lawyer advises them to keep up 'appearances' before the legal hearing so that neighbours will not be able to witness in any way against their behaviour. The following is Ginny's response to this advice.

I was so remarkably comfortable with the discipline of making a good appearance! It was like going back to school or church after a long absence. It had ritual and measure. Tasks proliferated. Once you made a good appearance your goal, you could confidently do things like nest all the spoons and forks in the newly washed and dried silverware tray and face them in the same direction. You could spend an hour or two vacuuming the tops of the floor moldings in the house with an attachment you'd never used before, then go back over what you'd done with a sponge dampened in ammonia, then again with furniture polish. There was cleaning you could do in the bathroom with an old toothbrush that might have repelled you before. There were corners and angles and seams all over the house that could be gotten at. The outside of the house itself could be scrubbed from a ladder, with the hose and a brush. The outside second-storey windows could be washed. The grass could be edged and trimmed and raked and rolled for the great open invisible eye of The Neighbors to judge and enjoy. Cars and trucks, of course, could be washed every day. There could be no limit to your schedule. Even though you had washed the supper dishes as you were cooking, you could jump up from the table when a serving dish

> *got emptied, and wash and dry it and put it away before finishing your beans. You could follow your husband from the door to the sink, and sweep the dust from his boots into the dustpan and throw it away before he was finished washing his hands, and then you could take the towel he had dried them with and run it downstairs to the washing machine while he was sitting down to his food.*

A marvellous paragraph, it proceeds from the probable to the possible and on into a fantasy of compulsive cleaning in which the wife, like a maniac or slave, or like a maniacal slave, cleans up her husband's footsteps as he walks. Its humour is caustic, self-lacerating and at this stage of the novel intensely revealing of character.

A few chapters on, however, what was fantasy becomes reality.

> *I finished the dishes, swept the floor, wiped the counter, cleaned the seams in the counter with a toothpick, scoured the drip pans and burner grates, applied the toothpick to the assorted corners of the stove, and cleaned the oven doors with Windex. These activities coalesced into a kind of waking dream that was punctuated by the rumble of the combines passing on the west side of the house.*

What in the first extract was presented as hypothetical – 'cleaning you *could* [my emphasis] do in the bathroom with an old toothbrush' – is now made to appear positively slovenly by Ginny downsizing her cleaning implement. She cleans 'the seams in the counter with a toothpick' and applies 'the toothpick to the assorted corners of the stove'.

And there's the nice touch by the writer to emphasize the contrast by the repeat of the word 'tooth' in the two implements. It would seem a more likely military punishment than household chore to clean a stove with a toothpick.

At the level of character development, at this stage of the novel you understand that none of Ginny's crazy cleaning will ever remove the filth she feels within, now that she's been forced to remember her father sexually abusing her for years in her childhood.

Work as action: coalmining

The motivation of work as a mark of respectability, opiate and hoped-for therapy against memory in *A Thousand Acres* – that is, social and psychological motivation – has little to do with late nineteenth-century coalmining in France, where motivation is rock-bottom basic – to keep from starving to death. This is the driving force in Émile Zola's masterpiece of 'naturalism' *Germinal*, published in 1885.

In the following extracts from the novel, the out-of-work engineer Étienne has just been taken on at the coalmine, never having done such work before. He is befriended by the young girl Catherine, who works there with her father, Maheu, and her older brother, Zacharie.

The four pikemen had spread themselves one above the other over the whole face of the cutting. Separated by planks, hooked on to retain the fallen coal, they each occupied about four metres of the seam, and this seam was so thin, scarcely more than fifty centimetres thick at this spot, that they seemed to be flattened between the roof and the wall, dragging themselves along by their knees and elbows, and unable to turn without crushing their shoulders. In order to attack the coal, they had to lie on their sides with their arms raised, brandishing, in a sloping direction, their short-handled picks.

Below there was, first, Zacharie; Levaque and Chaval were on the stages above, and at the very top was Maheu. Each worked at the slaty bed, which he dug out with blows of the pick; then he made two vertical cuttings in the bed and detached the block by burying an iron wedge in its upper part. The coal was rich; the block broke and rolled in fragments along their bellies and thighs. When these fragments, retained by the plank, had collected round them, the pikemen disappeared, buried in the narrow cleft.

Maheu suffered most. At the top the temperature rose to thirty-five degrees, and the air was stagnant, so that in the long run it became lethal. In order to see, he had been obliged to fix his lamp to a nail near his head, and this lamp, close to his skull, still further heated his blood. But his torment was especially aggravated by the moisture. The rock above him, a few centimetres from his face, streamed with water, which fell in large continuous rapid drops with a sort of obstinate rhythm, always at the same spot. It was

vain for him to twist his head or bend back his neck. They
fell on his face, dropping unceasingly. In a quarter of an
hour he was soaked, and at the same time covered with
sweat, smoking as with the hot steam of a laundry. This
morning a drop beating upon his eye made him swear.
He would not leave his picking, he dealt great strokes
which shook him violently between the two rocks, like a
fly caught between two leaves of a book and in danger of
being completely flattened.

Not a word was exchanged. They all hammered; one
only heard these irregular blows, which seemed veiled
and remote. The sounds had a sonorous hoarseness,
without any echo in the dead air. And it seemed that the
darkness was an unknown blackness, thickened by the
floating coal dust, made heavy by the gas which weighed
on the eyes. The wicks of the lamps beneath their caps
of metallic tissue only showed as reddish points. One
could distinguish nothing. The cutting opened out above
like a large chimney, flat and oblique, in which the soot
of ten years had amassed a profound night. Spectral
figures were moving in it, the gleams of light enabled
one to catch a glimpse of a rounded hip, a knotty arm, a
vigorous head, besmeared as if for a crime. Sometimes,
blocks of coal shone suddenly as they became detached,
illuminated by a crystalline reflection. Then everything
fell back into darkness, pickaxes struck great hollow
blows; one only heard panting chests, the grunting of
discomfort and weariness beneath the weight of the air
and the rain of the springs.

Notice how the action goes from a broader scene – the men dragging
themselves through the tiny coal seam – into close-up action of the
water dripping on Maheu's face, so that you feel the torment of a
particular person – the damp, the heat, the claustrophobic condition
that keeps him from avoiding this water torture. Maheu knows one
thing very well – that he must keep working to fulfil his quota of
coal if he wants to be paid, if he wants food, if he wants his family
and himself to survive.

Then the action switches to the newcomer Étienne.

Étienne, who was learning from Catherine how to manage his shovel, had to raise the wood in the cutting. A small supply had remained over from yesterday. It was usually sent down every morning cut to fit in the bed.

'Hurry up there, damn it!' shouted Zacharie, seeing the new putter hoist himself up awkwardly in the midst of the coal, his arms embarrassed by four pieces of oak.

He made a hole in the roof with his pickaxe, and then another in the wall, and wedged in the two ends of the wood, which thus supported the rock. In the afternoon the workers in the earth cutting took the rubbish left at the bottom of the gallery by the pikemen and cleared out the exhausted section of the seam, in which they destroyed the wood, being only careful about the lower and upper roads for the haulage.

Étienne is able to figure this out, but other tasks are more daunting:

The young man, whose eyes now became accustomed to the darkness, looked at her [Catherine], still white with her chlorotic complexion, and he could not have told her age; he thought she must be twelve, she seemed so slight. However, he felt she must be older, with her boyish freedom, a simple audacity which confused him a little; she did not please him: he thought her too roguish with her pale Pierrot head, framed at the temples by the cap. But what astonished him was the strength of this child, a nervous strength which was blended with a good deal of skill. She filled her tram faster than he could, with quick small regular strokes of the shovel; she afterwards pushed it to the inclined way with a single slow push, without a hitch, easily passing under the low rocks. He tore himself to pieces, got off the rails, and was reduced to despair.

It was certainly not a convenient road. It was sixty metres from the cutting to the upbrow, and the passage, which the miners in the earth cutting had not yet enlarged, was a mere tube with a very irregular roof swollen by innumerable bosses; at certain spots the laden tram could only just pass; the putter had to flatten himself, to push on his knees, in order not to break his head, and besides this the wood was already bending and yielding. One could see it broken in the middle in long pale rents like an over-weak crutch. One had to be careful not to graze oneself in these fractures; and beneath the slow crushing, which caused the splitting of billets of oak as large as the thigh, one had to glide almost on one's belly with a secret fear of suddenly hearing one's back break.

'Again!' said Catherine, laughing.

Étienne's tram had gone off the rails at the most difficult spot. He could not roll straight on these rails which sank in the damp earth, and he swore, became angry, and fought furiously with the wheels, which he could not get back into place in spite of exaggerated efforts.

'Wait a bit,' said the young girl. 'If you get angry it will never go.' Skilfully she had glided down, had thrust her buttocks beneath the tram, and by putting the weight on her loins she raised it and replaced it. The weight was seven hundred kilograms. Surprised and ashamed, he stammered excuses.

She was obliged to show him how to separate his legs to support his feet against the planking on both sides of the gallery, in order to give himself a more solid fulcrum. The body had to be bent, the arms made stiff so as to push with all the muscles of the shoulders and hips. During the journey he followed her and watched her proceed with tense back, her fists so low that she seemed trotting on all fours, like one of those dwarf beasts that perform at circuses. She sweated, panted, her joints cracked, but without a complaint, with the indifference of custom, as if it were the common wretchedness of all to live thus bent double. But he could not succeed in doing as much; his shoes troubled him, his body seemed broken by walking in this way with lowered head. At the end of a few minutes the position became a torture, an intolerable anguish, so painful that he got on his knees for a moment to straighten himself and breathe.

Here, Zola breaks off from individual actions for a few paragraphs and returns to describing group actions around the coalface. Then he picks up Étienne:

> *And on each journey Étienne found again at the bottom the stuffiness of the cutting, the hollow and broken cadence of the axes, the deep painful sighs of the pikemen persisting in their work. All four were naked, mixed up with the coal, soaked with black mud up to the cap. At one moment it had been necessary to free Maheu, who was gasping, and to remove the planks so that the coal could fall into the passage. Zacharie and Lavaque became enraged with the seam, which was now hard, they said, and which would make the condition of their account disastrous. Chaval turned, lying for a moment on his back, abusing Étienne, whose presence decidedly exasperated him.*
>
> *'A sort of worm; hasn't the strength of a girl! Are you going to fill your tub? It's to spare your arms, eh? Damned if I don't keep back the ten sous if you get us one refused!'*
>
> *The young man avoided replying, too happy at present to have found this convict's labour and accepting the brutal rule of the worker by master worker. But he could no longer walk, his feet were bleeding, his limbs torn by horrible cramps, his body confined in an iron girdle.*

Reading this as a writer, you'll be aware that Étienne 'works' in several ways for the novel. First, of course, he's a main character, perhaps the main character. Then, as an outsider, his point of view enables reader identification as he learns the working and social culture of the mining community. And physically, you, almost all or all of you, are – like him – not coalminers and so you imaginatively connect with Étienne's exhaustion, pain, and near disbelief that anyone, let alone a young, skinny girl, could survive such unrelentingly gruelling labour.

You can imagine yourself knowing enough or easily learning enough about house cleaning to write your own version of Smiley's character's obsessive cleaning, from vacuum to scrub brush to toothbrush to toothpick, but what about coalmining? Coalmining in late nineteenth-century France? You know the answer, of course: the Internet. Zola wasn't a coalminer, so he had to take a notebook, go out to the French/Belgian coalmining district, and spend six months there down the mines, around the mines, and in the cafés and houses of the coalminers asking questions, noting down everything. Of course, Zola had the advantage of writing about contemporary work. But even if you wanted to write about coalmining today and only used the Internet or books to do the research, you'd still understand that nothing could substitute for you actually going down into a mine and getting to the coalface to see how its worked. Yes, you could see it online, but could you feel the heat? Smell the air? The damp? Maybe the gas?

On the other hand, this doesn't mean you couldn't write it convincingly, for fiction is above all created from your imagination as well as your memory.

The last two examples of work as action have been emotionally negative: work as a mask of normality and as obsessive means of repressing truth; and then work as drudgery, as physical torture and means of bare subsistence. But there is also work that fiction represents as positive – mentally, physically and psychologically.

The emphasis here on work as action developing character comes from my own reading of a range of contemporary and late twentieth-century fiction, in which there has been relatively little work portrayed. An exception to this is the work of writing – writers writing about writers writing – often satirically, almost always ironically. (Another notable exception is the physical and administrative work in crime genre fiction, especially in police procedurals.)

Work as action: milking

Philip Roth is one writer for whom non-writing work is typically treated as socially and personally positive, so that characters described at work become endowed with positive attributes not necessarily manifested at other times in the particular novel. Here, from his 2000 novel *The Human Stain,* the narrator, writer Nathan Zuckerman, and his neighbour and new friend Coleman Silk, the novel's protagonist, watch Silk's new girlfriend, Faunia Farley, half Silk's age, at work in a dairy.

> We stood there watching while she milked each of the eleven cows – Daisy, Maggie, Flossie, Bessy, Dolly, Maiden, Sweetheart, Stupid, Emma, Friendly and Jill – stood there while she went through the same unvarying routine with every one of them, and when that was finished and she moved into the whitewashed room with the big sinks

and the hoses and the sterilizing units adjacent to the
milking parlor, we watched her through that doorway
mixing up the lye solution and the cleansing agents and,
after separating the vacuum line from the pipeline and
the teat cups from the claw and the two milk pails from
their covers – after disassembling the whole of the milking
unit that she'd taken in there with her – settling to work
with a variety of brushes and with sinkful after sinkful
of clear water to scrub every surface of every tube, valve,
gasket, plug, plate, liner, cap, disc, and piston until each
was spotlessly clean and sanitized. Before Coleman took
his milk and we got back into his car to leave, he and
I had stood together by the refrigerator for close to an
hour and a half and, aside from the words he uttered to
introduce me to her, nobody human said anything more.
All you could hear was the whirring and the chirping of the
barn swallows who nested there as they whished through
the rafters where the barn opened out behind us, and the
pellets dropping into the cement trough when she shook
out the feed pail, and the shuffling clump of the barely
lifted hooves on the milking parlor floor as Faunia, shoving
and dragging and steering the cows, positioned them into
the stanchion, and then the suction noise, the soft deep
breathing of the milk pump.

Never mind that Faunia ran away from home at fourteen, waited
on tables, was propositioned by customers for one-night stands,
to be their mistress, to be their whore and get rich, refused and
finds herself with two small children and maybe has whored
herself to support them, has married a crazed, violent Vietnam vet
for whom she's pretended to be illiterate so that he'll feel superior
to her – forget all that, because as you watch and listen to her
working with the cows you sense she's clear-headed, responsible
and fully human. As a writer, you should look closely at the long
passage of visual imagery followed by a long passage of aural
imagery, at details like the naming of each of the eleven cows
and the sounds of the barn swallows, to see how Roth brings
life and beauty and great respect into the action, lifting it from a
mere list of bits of machinery. And, come to that, you should also
note his care to name everything in the breakdown and cleaning
of the actual machinery, so that the human feelings evoked are
grounded in the actual.

Work as action: glove making

In Roth's 1997 novel *American Pastoral,* the protagonist Swede (Seymour) Levov, struggling to understand the seeming inversion of human values in the society around him and particularly in his own beloved daughter, recalls with pleasure his father passing on to him, as a boy, his love of work as a glove manufacturer.

On Saturday mornings, the Swede would drive Down Neck alongside his father to pick up the week's finished gloves from the Italian families paid to do piecework in their homes. As the car bounced along the streets paved with bricks, past one poor little frame house after another, the massive railroad viaduct remained brokenly within view. It would not go away. This was the Swede's first encounter with the manmade sublime that divides and dwarfs, and in the beginning it was frightening to him, a child susceptible to his environment even then, with a proclivity to be embraced by it and to embrace it in return. Six or seven years old. ...

His father didn't even have a loft there but got his skins from a fellow who was also Down Neck and who trafficked out of his garage in whatever the workers could carry from the tanneries hidden within their big rubber boots or wrapped around them beneath their overalls. The hide man was himself a tannery worker, a big, gruff Pole with tattoos up and down his massive arms, and the Swede had vague memories of his father's standing at the garage's one window holding the finished hides up to the light and searching them for defects, then stretching them over his knee before making his selection. 'Feel this,' he'd say to the Swede once they were safely back in the car, and the child would crease a delicate kidskin as he'd seen his father do, finger the fineness appreciatively, the velvet texture of the skin's tight grain. 'That's leather,' his father told him. 'What makes kidskin so delicate, Seymour?' 'I don't know.' 'Well, what is a kid?' 'A baby goat.' 'Right. And what does he eat?' 'Milk?' 'Right. And because all the animal has eaten is milk, that's what makes the grain smooth and beautiful. Look at the pores of this skin with a magnifying glass and they're so fine you can't even see 'em. But the kid starts eating grass, that skin's a different story. The goat eats grass

101

and the skin is like sandpaper. The finest glove leather for a formal glove is what, Seymour?' 'Kid.' 'That's my boy. But it's not only the kid, son, it's the tanning. You've got to know your tannery. It's like a good cook and a bad cook. ... I worked in the tannery. It's the chemicals, it's the time, it's the temperature. That's where the difference comes in. That, and not buying second-rate skins to begin with. Cost as much to tan a bad skin as a good skin. Cost more to tan a bad one – you work harder at it. Beautiful, beautiful,' he said, 'wonderful stuff,' once again lovingly kneading the kidskin between his fingertips. 'You know how you get it like this, Seymour?' 'How, Daddy?' 'You work at it.'

The first segment of the extract sets the scene for these nostalgic memories. The key to the Swede's love of work is not just his memory of the facts about glove leather and its tanning, but his recreating the feeling for his father, the bonding in the cosy privacy of the car, the Piranesi-like imagery of the industrial cityscape under that spell of loving intimacy. Though the second section is substantially in dialogue – a tender question and answer conversation – it is inseparable from the bonding, from the lesson in leather and love, of its enthusiasm and encouragement. In this way the father's speech becomes a narrative in retrospect of the pleasure of his work as tenderly inculcated by his son.

Roth's father was neither dairyman nor glove maker. He sold insurance. Roth did grow up in such a place (Newark, New Jersey). You need a feel for what you write, but it doesn't have to be literally sourced in your life. The point is that you have experienced things. You know things; you remember details. You apply the facts you need to find to the world of the fiction you're writing; you make that world feel factual even though its facts are fictional. What binds the two in the extracts above is the emotional truth of the writing.

Write a work-as-action scene

Write a 750-word action scene in which the action is work of some kind. Choose work with which you are either familiar or which interests you and which you'd like to learn more about via online research or by interview (with a family member or friend, etc.). The work may be presented positively or negatively, but remember that either way it must develop the character you're writing about. You may, of course, use a character that already exists in your portfolio.

Short action

The action excerpted in this chapter has mostly been part of extended action scenes. But much action in fiction is much shorter, itself part of a longer scene where narrative of other sorts or where dialogue is dominant.

In the following pieces of short action, the same initial motive, sometimes referred to as a 'spring of action', sets the action going.

1 Barbara clicked the phone off. All right, she thought, he can't make it home tonight. The bad weather's not his fault. And he managed to get the gift delivered. She looked at the package, still unwrapped. From its size she had a good idea it was what she'd wanted. She could imagine the Meissen figures within, their fine white arms wrapped round each other. He'd managed that. She thought about 'managed that', not a kind way to put it, not, certainly, a loving way. She picked up the package thinking to unwrap it, and walked into the bedroom to sit on the bed. Instead, she found herself at the closet door, still looking at the wrapped anniversary present, asking herself how hard, really, was that to manage? She opened the closet door, pushed the hanging clothes apart, pulled out the stool and stepping up she placed the package at the back of the top shelf, among other things no longer wanted but impossible to get rid of.

2 Barbara clicked the phone off and set it on the counter. The weather, he said. That's what he was calling it this time. She looked at the Meissen figures, the entwined lovers. What she'd wanted for her birthday, eighteenth century, and it must have cost him a lot. It cost him nothing, really. Less than that. She touched it lightly with her finger on the man's white shoulders. She pushed it and it fell off the counter and smashed to pieces on the kitchen floor.

3 Barbara clicked off the phone. Okay, so he couldn't make it back tonight, poor Jimmy. She took his present into the living room, put it on the coffee table and sat on the sofa. It was sweet of him, sweet and extravagant. She didn't even want to imagine what it cost. He'd had to go all the way out to that little place and buy it and have it wrapped and then he'd had to set up the delivery. Poor Jimmy, stuck out in the middle of nowhere now. She picked up the gorgeous figurine and held the cold white lovers to her cheek.

The first piece, above, suggests a certain reserved resignation to the situation. It also suggests some collusion on Barbara's part and even a metaphor, of sorts, of action: the putting away of what she wants, or a slightly masochistic self-denial. Nevertheless, it serves as her rejection of him, a rejection of his rejection of her.

The Barbara of the second piece is very different. She knows what he's up to, she's on to him. The thousands, the tens of thousands it cost don't really mean anything to him. Screw him, screw his lovers. His lovers! She smashes him and his lovers to bits.

The third Barbara is perhaps younger, newer in her relationship. Jimmy may be telling the truth. Barbara may not be naive. There may be no irony in the piece, though the 'cold' porcelain is no real substitute for Jimmy.

Write a short-action piece

Write your own version or versions of this idea in about 350 words, total. Rename the characters but begin with your character putting the phone down after receiving the same sort of message from her/his partner or lover or spouse. Make the small action telling in the characterization.

Workshop

Is writing scenes of action or pieces of short action any easier or more difficult for you to write than other elements of fiction such as non-action narrative or dialogue? If it is more difficult, can you look at some examples to try to understand why this is? For instance, does it read as stiff and awkward? Check that you've cut out all words and phrases that aren't vital to the action. What about too many adverbs? A really vivid verb can be better than a number of adverbs trying to put life into too abstract or overused a verb.

- Does the action in your writing, long or short, develop your character(s)? Will giving more conscious thought to this in rewriting and/or editing help that development?
- Action has nearly no limits in type. Do certain types of action tend to dominate the example of action in your writing? What are they? (This chapter has given some examples, but has had to leave out many important types, for example, actions connected with eating and

lovemaking.) Do you think your fiction could improve if you ventured out of your 'favourite' areas of action?

- What sort of work, as action, occurs in your writing? If none or very little, can you validate its omission? How much of the action that's descriptive of work in your writing comes from your own experience? How much has been researched?
- If you're an urban or a suburban type (statistically, most of us writers) and there was a rural, farming character of importance to the piece of fiction you were working on, what would you do to feel comfortable with 'knowing' this character's background?
- If you don't care two beans about, say, farming, what might you do to change your attitude about writing about it? Would you simply ignore it and have your fiction leave it as a mysterious or stupid or yokel or hick topic for your characters? Ask yourself the same question about sports as action, and, come to that, sports as work.

Focus points

- In writing fiction, showing a character in action is a direct way of engaging the reader in the interior life and development of a character.
- A slow-action scene is finely detailed and often small in scale.
- A quick-action scene carries the reader along quickly, using racy, racing language; it leaves him or her curious to know more about the character or characters.
- Showing a scene of action, long or short, fast or slow, is important to the development of character.
- Action includes the character's physical actions as well as dialogue.

Next step

The next chapter presents the other major way of 'showing' character rather than 'telling' it – dialogue. This will be looked at both in scenes of dialogue and in short dialogue within other types of scene.

6

Showing character through dialogue

So much of what makes us human resides in our ability to speak with each other. This makes speech in fiction – dialogue – a naturally powerful way of showing character.

In an earlier book I wrote for the Teach Yourself series, *How to Write Dialogue in Fiction*, I began with a statement of definition followed by one of distinction. 'Dialogue in fiction is the written representation of speech between two or more people. Dialogue in real life is the speech between two or more people.' The distinction is worth making. Even the use of 'found' dialogue cannot go on in fiction for very long without authorial interventions such as selection, omissions, additions and rearrangement.

Dialogue in fiction may be presented in a variety of formats and in variable amounts; the only rule is that it has to work. It has to be interesting, further the story and develop the characters.

Formatting dialogue

Today, dialogue in fiction may be presented in a variety of recognizable formats; you only need some consistency of format in any one work of fiction to signal dialogue. But the earliest writers of fiction in English were undecided on dialogue's presentation. Here's dialogue from Daniel Defoe's *A Journal of the Plague Year*, published in 1722.

> *Says John the Biscuit Baker one Day to Thomas his brother, the Sail Maker.*
>
> *Brother Tom, what will become of us? The Plague grows hot in the City, and encreases this way. What shall we do?*
>
> *Truly, says Thomas, I am at a great loss what to do, for I find, if it comes down into Wapping, I shall be turn'd out of my lodging...*
>
> *John: Turn'd out of your lodging, Tom? If you are, I don't know who will take you in; for People are so afraid of one another now, there's no getting a lodging anywhere.*
>
> *Tho: Why? The People where I lodge are good civil People, and have kindness enough for me too...*

The first two exchanges are recognizable as one way we signal dialogue today, with its identifying narrative 'says Thomas'. But the second two switch into the convention of a play script, with each new speaker's name preceding the dialogue. By the end of the eighteenth century, the conventions that now exist had been normalized and by the middle of the nineteenth century there were strict conventions for presenting dialogue in fiction. Indeed, by this time they had become so rigid that the appearance of Herman Melville's novel *Moby Dick* in 1862, with its return in some chapters to presenting dialogue as in a play, was, along with other aspects of the novel, held to be unfathomable. Here's the opening of the operatic Chapter XL.

> *CHAPTER XL MIDNIGHT, FORECASTLE*
>
> [Foresail rises, and discovers the watch standing, lounging, leaning, and lying in various attitudes, all singing in chorus]
>
> Farewell and adieu to you, Spanish ladies!
>
> Farewell and adieu to you, ladies of Spain!

Our captain's commanded. –

1ST NANTUCKET SAILOR

Oh, boys, don't be sentimental; it's bad for the digestion!
Take a tonic, follow me!

[Sings, and all follow]

Our captain stood upon the deck,

A spy-glass in his hand,

A viewing of those gallant whales

That blew at every strand.

Oh, your tubs in your boats, my boys,

And by your braces stand,

And we'll have one of those fine whales,

Hand, boys, over hand!

So be cheery, my lads! may your hearts never fail!

While the bold harpooner is striking the whale!

MATE'S VOICE FROM THE QUARTER-DECK

Eight bells there, forward!

2ND NANTUCKET SAILOR

Avast the chorus! Eight bells there! d'ye hear, bell-boy?
Strike the bell eight, thou Pip! thou blackling! and let
me call the watch. I've the sort of mouth for that – the
hogshead mouth. So, so (thrusts his head down the
scuttle), *Star-bo-l-e-e-n-s, a-h-o-y! Eight bells there below!*
Tumble up!

DUTCH SAILOR

Grand snoozing to-night, matey; fat night for that. I mark
this in our old Mogul's wine; it's quite as deadening to
some as filliping to others. We sing; they sleep – aye, lie
down there, like ground-tier butts. At 'em again! There,
take this copper-pump, and hail 'em through it. Tell 'em
it's the resurrection; they must kiss their last, and come
to judgement. That's the way – that's it; thy throat ain't
spoiled with eating Amsterdam butter.

Hist, boys! let's have a jig or two before we ride to anchor in Blanket Bay. What say ye? There comes the other watch. Stand by all legs! Pip! Hurrah with your tambourine!

Amount of dialogue

Not only can dialogue format vary greatly (though mainstream conventions are still generally kept), but the proportion of dialogue in any two pieces of fiction may be widely, wildly different.

Here's a typical page from Ivy Compton-Burnett's 1941 novel **Parents and Children**:

'How soon are you going away?' said Gavin, to his father.

'In about seven days.'

'That is a week,' said Honor.

'All night, all night,' said Nevill, beating his hand on his mother's knee.

'Yes, yes, all night. Honor, talk nicely to Father about his going. Tell him how you will miss him.'

Honor began to cry. Fulbert put his arm around her; Nevill gave her a look of respectful concern; Gavin surveyed her with a frown.

'There, dry your eyes and don't lean against Father,' said Eleanor. 'He is as tired as you are, at the end of the day. She was hiding her feelings, poor child.'

'She didn't hide them,' said Gavin.

'She tried to; she did not want to upset Father. You mind about his going too, don't you?'

'If we say we mind, he knows,' said Gavin, who was successfully hiding his own jealousy of his sister's interest.

'Father will be going away. Gallop-a-trot,' said Nevill, illustrating this idea of progress.

'Nevill doesn't know much,' said Gavin.

'Well, he is only three,' said Eleanor. 'Neither did you at that age.'

'Father come back soon,' said Nevill, showing his grasp of the situation.

'I think I knew more,' said Gavin.

'We shall expect good reports of your lessons, if you talk like that.'

'It is boys at school who have reports,' said Gavin, mindful of James's experience.

'Mother meant a verbal report,' said Honor, causing her parents to smile.

'You will soon be able to go to school,' said Eleanor, to her son. *'You won't always have a governess.'*

'James sometimes has Miss Mitford. I could always have her.'

'Do you mean you want to learn with Honor?'

'No,' said Gavin, true to his principle that real feeling should be hidden.

You could open just about any page of this or other Ivy Compton-Burnett novels and find the same preponderance of dialogue.

A few years later, in 1944, Jorge Luis Borges's volume of short stories **Fictions** appeared. Seven of its eight stories have not a word of dialogue. Borges's writing influenced many writers in, among other ways, creating fiction with little or no dialogue. A notable example of this is the black-humour bibliographic novel by the Chilean Roberto Bolano, **Nazi Literature in the Americas**, a novel without dialogue.

While Compton-Burnett's dialogue-rich and Borges's dialogue-light fiction are consistent enough to be marks of their styles, other good fiction writers are more flexible in how much dialogue they include in any particular work. Ian McEwan, for instance, has very little dialogue in his novel **Chesil Beach**, but this is significant to the subject and theme of his story of the courtship and wedding night of two middle-class, educated and sexually ignorant virgins who have grown up in the 1950s and early 1960s in England. They are shy, inhibited and tongue-tied, and the resulting awkwardness between them when they attempt to communicate by language and then by touch leads to greater and greater misunderstanding – lust in the groom and revulsion in the bride – that culminates in a final verbal outburst – the book's only extended dialogue – which drives them miserably apart. But this sparseness of dialogue is not typical, not a stylistic feature of McEwan's writing.

Key idea

There is only one rule about the format or the amount of dialogue that should or can appear in fiction: it has to work. It has to show basic human action, be interesting, further the story and develop the characters.

Using language to convey character

Kevin Power's Iraq War novel *The Yellow Birds* (2012) tells the story of John Bartle and his US army buddy Murph and the effect of their war experiences on them and their families. Murph goes mad and dies in Iraq; Bartle cannot forgive himself for letting this happen, because he's tried to look after Murph, an 18-year-old from an Appalachian mountain community, naive and kind, unable to be cynical and emotionally shut down enough to survive what they do and witness in the war. The extract below is from a scene at Fort Dix, New Jersey, where both boys' mothers have come to an army ceremony before their sons fly off to Iraq.

Most of the families had gone by then. Most but Murph's mother and a few others I didn't know. I saw Murph leading her by the hand throughout the gymnasium, investigating each small cluster of remaining people briefly, then moving on. I didn't realize they were looking for me until Murph turned in my direction and I saw him mouth something to his mother. I got up from the chair where I'd been sitting and waited for them to cross over the painted lines of the basketball court that had been used for our festivities.

Mrs LaDonna Murphy hugged me tightly when I met her. She was small and frail-looking in a weathered sort of way, but younger than my mother. She smiled broadly when she looked at me, still wrapping her arms around my waist, looking up and showing me teeth slightly browned by smoke. Her hair was a faded blond worn in a bun, and she had on jeans and a blue button-up work shirt.

'Five more minutes, men,' one of the NCOs called.

She released me from her embrace and said excitedly, 'I'm just so proud of you guys. Daniel's told me so much about you. I feel like I know you already.'

'Yes, ma'am. Me too.'

'So y'all are getting to be good friends?'

I looked over at Murph and he gave me an apologetic shrug. 'Yes, ma'am,' I said. 'We room together and everything.'

'Well, I want you to know if y'all need anything, I'm gonna take care of you. Y'all will get more care packages than anyone.'

'That's really kind of you, Mrs. Murphy.'

Sterling called Murph to help another private sweep up red, white and blue confetti from around the three-point line of the court.

'And you're gonna look out for him, right?' she asked.

'Um, yes, ma'am.'

'And Daniel, he's doing a good job?'

'Yes, ma'am, very good.' How the hell should I know, lady? I wanted to say. I barely knew the guy. Stop. Stop asking me questions. I don't want to be accountable. I don't know anything about this.

'John, promise me that you'll take care of him.'

'Of course.' Sure, sure, I thought. Now you reassure me and I'll go back to bed.

'Nothing's gonna happen to him, right? Promise that you'll bring him home to me.'

'I promise,' I said. 'I promise I'll bring him home to you.'

This dialogue scene sounds right to you: clear, direct and simple. That's as it should be, but because *writing it* is neither direct nor simple, its clarity is also not so easily achieved.

The first thing to notice is that the dialogue is entirely between John and Mrs Murphy. Although her son is present during half the length of the dialogue, he says nothing, merely shrugs once. Then you notice that there are questions and statements, and if you count

Mrs Murphy's two demands ('Promise me...', 'Promise that...'), she asks all six of them. John only responds. He responds politely, but it's Murph's mother who creates the dialogue; she's the active character, John's passive. You also see that while her son is there, Mrs Murphy acts like a mother to both Murph and John. But once Murph (Daniel) is called away, she's single-minded in deputizing John to look after her son, to be *in loco parentis*, her son's guardian in the war.

The language in the dialogue is clear and direct from both characters, but there are subtle and significant differences in diction. Mrs Murphy uses the southern (US) dialect 'y'all' to refer to more than one in the second person. Note, however, that she doesn't do this all the time: 'Well, I want *you* to know if *y'all* need anything, I'm gonna take care of *you*. *Y'all* will get more care packages than anyone [my emphasis].' This is more realistic than having a southern character using it all the time. The term has friendly and familial connotations. But you find that once her son is gone, once, that is, she gets down to the business she intends, she stops using it. This makes for a small but powerful shift in her tone. She is, after all, not John's mother but only Daniel's mother. She's also a contemporary American character and sounds like one when she says, 'I'm just so proud of *you guys* [my emphasis].' Finally, you see that her southern accent isn't overdone; Powers doesn't have her say 'Ah'm' for 'I'm', and so on. A suggestion of accent goes a long way. Her speech rushes out in a contemporary mix of American diction, becoming less or more formal as her intentions in speaking change.

John Bartle's speech is slightly more formal, partly politeness for someone he's just met who's the mother of an acquaintance (not really a close friend), and sometimes indicative of a different social background. But since you've already heard him speak as the first-person narrator, you'll be aware of how articulate and imaginatively exact his language can be, so when you read 'We room together and everything', you hear that last word as an extemporized lie, though not a literal one, to her question suggesting he's 'good friends' with Murph. In this context, 'everything' is consciously inarticulate, a mumble masquerading as a word. But he says to her, 'That's really kind of you', rather then 'That's real kind of you', and this second-nature use of the adverb implies his education and literacy. He answers all her questions, outwardly polite to Mrs Murphy. But his unspoken thoughts reveal that his politeness is merely polite.

His promise to Mrs Murphy is made against his will – it makes him accountable. This is the moral crux of the plot. Its importance is emphasized when John walks away towards his barracks immediately after this promise to bring Murph home to her, and he runs into his and Murph's squad sergeant, Sterling, who tells him he's overheard this promise.

> *'You shouldn't have done that, Private.'*
>
> *'What?'*
>
> *He stopped and put his hands on his hips. 'C'mon. Promises? Really? You're making fucking promises now?'*
>
> *I was annoyed: 'I was just trying to make her feel better, Sarge,' I said. 'It's not a big deal.'*
>
> *He knocked me to the ground quickly and hit me twice on the face, once below my eye and once directly in the mouth. I felt his knuckles fold my lips under my teeth. I felt my front teeth cut into my top lip, the blood running hot and metallic into my mouth. My lip swelled immediately. My cheek had been cut by a ring he wore on his right hand, and that blood gathered into runnels and ran down my face and into the corner of my eye and on to the snow. He stood over me with his feet on either side of my body, just looking at me. He shook the sting out of his hand in the cold air. 'Report me if you want. I don't even fucking care anymore.'*

Sterling, a battle-scarred veteran physically and emotionally, knows better than to make impossible promises. This promise was made to make John feel better, not Murph's mother. The effect of such promises when impossible to keep is to make mothers and families back home even more miserable than they will be when hearing of the death of sons or husbands or brothers. But this isn't what makes him hit John. It's John's casual 'It's not a big deal' that enrages the violent sergeant. It is a big deal – a deeply selfish, immoral big deal.

This takes place in the novel's second chapter. From its first chapter, you know that Murph has been killed. The novel's plot revolves around the physical and emotional implications of this promise that John is unable to keep; the novel's theme develops out of the moral implications. This is a powerful example of dialogue as a basic human action, a means of showing and thereby developing character.

Use an accent in a dialogue

Write a 300-word, two-character dialogue in which one character speaks English with an accent. If you're familiar with a particular accent and/or dialect you can use it. In any case, try to suggest it rather than laying it on too heavily.

Using dialogue within descriptive narrative

The plot of Ann Patchett's 2001 novel **Bel Canto** makes some relatively unusual demands on its dialogue. When a group of wealthy and powerful business and political figures attending a party at the home of the vice-president of a Latin American country become hostages there to an armed group of revolutionaries, the house is immediately besieged by government troops. Negotiations between the government and the insurgents begin and continue for month after month. At first, the hostage guests are not allowed to speak at all. But as the siege and negotiations become protracted and the rebels' rules are relaxed, relationships develop not only among those held hostage but between the hostages and their captors.

This is the microcosmic setting, a little world sealed off from the big world outside. The people inside are for the most part strangers to one another. Two of the characters, however, are known by reputation to all the guests at the party: Katsumi Hosokama, for whose birthday the government throws the party, is the Japanese electronics mogul it hopes will open electronic factories in its country. The second is the American soprano Roxanne Coss, to whom the government has paid an enormous fee to sing at the party, her presence being the only draw powerful enough to bring Hosokawa, not only an opera buff but a most dedicated fan of Roxanne Coss, whom he has never met. To the frustration of the rebels, the president of the country has decided at the last moment not to attend the party so that he can stay at home in his bedroom to watch a climactic instalment of his favourite TV soap opera.

Since the rebels' plan to capture the president has come to nothing, they decide that their only chance to achieve this now is to negotiate a trade of the most important hostages for him. The rebels let all the sick men and all the women except one leave the premises. It's Roxanne, of course, who's kept, along with Hosokawa and the other men, all of them powerful. Those remaining are from many countries;

few speak foreign languages so they require a translator to converse. This, of course, sets another particular condition on the dialogue. Mr Hosokawa, who speaks only Japanese, has brought along his own translator, Gen Watanabe. Another translator present some of the time is Joachim Messner, a Swiss Red Cross mediator taking messages between the rebels and the government authorities. He speaks several European languages besides English. The following scene has both translators working together in the presence of General Alfredo, one of the rebel leaders. The general speaks only Spanish.

> *Messner took the papers and scanned them for a minute and then asked Gen to read them. Gen was surprised to find his hands trembling. He could never remember an instance when what he was translating had actually affected him.*
>
> *'On behalf of the people, La Familia de Martin Suarez has taken hostage –'*
>
> *Messner raised his hand for Gen to stop. 'La Familia de Martin Suarez?'*
>
> *The General nodded.*
>
> *'Not La Dirección Auténtica?' Messner kept his voice down.*
>
> *'You said we were* reasonable *men,' General Alfredo said, his voice swelling with the insult. 'What do you think? Do you think La Dirección Auténtica would be talking to you? Do you think we would be letting the women go? I know LDA. In LDA, the ones who are not useful are shot. Who have we shot? We are trying to do something for the people, can you understand that?' He took a step towards Messner, who knew how it was intended, but Gen moved quietly between them.*
>
> *'We are trying to do something for the people,' Gen said, keeping his tone deliberate and slow. The second part of the sentence, 'Can you understand that?' was irrelevant and so he left it off.*

This scene's dialogue dramatically demonstrates the difference between the amateur translator Messner's attitude and that of a professional. Messner's personal assumption that the hostage takers were a rival group to La Familia creates an impasse in the negotiations. When Gen, the professional translator, steps in, he takes care not to translate the most aggressive part of General Alfredo's response. He doesn't even think of his omission as diplomatic, he considers it merely 'irrelevant'. This calm, intelligent response is part of the author's development of Gen as a basically good, as well as major, character.

The scene is also representative of Patchett's approach to dialogue in this novel. Generally, the dialogue scenes contain at least as much descriptive narrative and narration of inner thought and feeling as dialogue itself. This is different from Powers' approach in the previous example, in which dialogue scenes tend to contain more dialogue than narrative, the bulk of the narrative being presented before and after the dialogue.

In *Bel Canto*, where a scene of dialogue occurs with a minor character who hasn't yet had much mention, the scene is introduced with substantial descriptive narrative about her or his background so that the dialogue can then proceed relatively unencumbered with exposition. Beatriz is one such character you'll have learned about in this way, a very serious revolutionary, a native-speaking Indian for whom Spanish is a poorly spoken second language. Out of boredom, she decides to go to confession in the dining room with Father Arguedas, a priest who has volunteered, literally insisted, to be held with the hostages. Beatriz has been listening to the confession before hers, lying outside the dining-room door where the priest can't see her.

> *'Come in now and make your confession. You have something to confess already. That will make it easier.' Father Arguedos was bluffing. None of the terrorists made confession, although many of them came to mass and he let them take communion just the same. He thought it was probably a rule of the Generals, no confession.*
>
> *But Beatriz had never made confession before. In her village, the priest came through irregularly, only when his schedule permitted it. The priest was a very busy man who served a large region in the mountains. Sometimes months would pass between visits and then when he came his time was crowded up with not only the mass itself but baptisms and marriages, funerals, land disputes, communion. Confession was saved for murderers and the terminally ill, not idle girls who had done nothing worse than pinch their sisters or disobey their mothers. It was something for the very grown up and for the very wicked, and if she were to tell the truth, Beatriz considered herself to be neither of those things.*

117

Father Arguedas held out his hand and he spoke to her softly. Really, he was the only one who ever spoke to her in that tone. 'Come here,' he said. 'I'll make this very easy for you.'

It was so simple to go to him, to sit down in the chair. He told her to bow her head and then he put a hand on either side of the straight part of her hair and began to pray for her. She didn't listen to the prayer. She only heard words here and there, beautiful words, father and blessed and forgiveness. It was just such a pleasant sensation, the weight of his hands on her head. When he finally took his hands away after what seemed to her a very long time, she felt delightfully weightless, free. She lifted up her face and smiled at him.

'Now you call your sins to mind,' he said. 'Usually you do that before you come. You pray to God to give you the courage to remember your sins and the courage to release them. And when you come to the confessional you say, "Bless me, Father, for I have sinned. This is my first confession."'

'Bless me, Father, for I have sinned. This is my first confession.'

Father Arguedas waited for a while but Beatriz only continued to smile at him. "Now you tell me your sins.'

'What are they?'

'Well,' he said, 'to start with, you listened in on Mr Mendoza's confession when you know it was the wrong thing to do.'

She shook her head. 'That wasn't a sin. I told you, I was doing my job.'

Father Arguedas put his hands on her shoulders this time and it had the same wonderfully calming effect on her. 'While you are in confession you must tell the absolute truth. You are telling that truth to God through me, and I will never tell another living soul. What this is is between you and me and God. It is a sacred rite and you must never, never lie when you make your confession. Do you understand that?'

'I do,' Beatriz whispered. He had the nicest face of anyone here, even nicer than Gen's, who she had liked a little bit before. All the other hostages were too old, and the boys in her troop were too young, and the Generals were the Generals.

'Pray,' the priest said. 'Try very hard to understand this.'

Because she liked him, she tried to make herself think about it. With the feel of his hands on her shoulders she closed her eyes and she prayed, and suddenly it seemed very clear to her. Yes, she knew she was not supposed to listen. She knew it like something she could see behind her closed eyes and it made her happy. 'I confess having listened.' All she had to do was say it and there it went, floating away from her. It wasn't her sin anymore.

'And something else?'

Something else. She thought again. She stared hard into the darkness of her closed eyes, the place where she knew the sins stacked up like kindling, dry and ready for a fire. There was something else, lots of something else. She began to see them all. But it was too much and she didn't know what to call it, how to form so many sins into words. 'I shouldn't have pointed the gun,' she said finally, because there was no way to make sense of it all. She felt like if she stayed forever she would never be able to confess them all. Not that she meant to stop doing any of those things. She couldn't stop. It wouldn't be allowed and she didn't even want to. She could see her sins now and knew that she would make more and more of them.

'God forgives you,' the priest said.

Beatriz opened her eyes and blinked at the priest. 'So it will go away?'

'You'll have to pray. You'll have to be sorry.'

'I can do that.' Maybe that was the answer, a sort of cycle of sinning and sorriness. She could come every Saturday, maybe more often than that, and he would keep having God forgive her, and then she would be free to go to heaven.

'I want you to say some prayers now.'

'I don't know all the words.'

Father Arguedas nodded his head. 'We can say them together. I can teach them to you. But, Beatriz, I need you to be kind, to be helpful. That is part of your contrition. I want you to try it just for today.'

The humour and charm of this scene are created by showing the difference between what Beatriz says and what she thinks; she's a fast learner, although, of course, she continually misses the point. The comic irony doesn't reside in Beatriz; it's an irony of character that involves you understanding what she doesn't about her view of confession, that it allows her to sin and wipe that sin away in the confessional, again and again. The irony is gentle because the tone of the dialogue is gentle. As the reader does, Father Arguedas understands that she doesn't quite get it, so you follow the scene along identifying with his point of view. And since he is consoling and literally forgiving with her, this tends to be your attitude towards Beatriz, too.

You also see that the mood of the scene and its dialogue contrasts greatly with the sombre, life-threatening atmosphere of much of the novel, so that such light moments underscore the existential fragility of those in the house – captive and captor alike.

A special challenge to dialogue is the situation of the novel's two main characters not speaking a word of each other's language. Yet the opera star Roxanne Coss and the businessman Katsumi Hosokawa fall in love during their enforced confinement together. Much of their growing mutual attraction is developed by fine narrative description of Coss's extraordinarily beautiful voice and Hosokawa's response to it. Everyone is taken with her singing and many men are enamoured with her, the only woman hostage, but the narrative tracks Roxanne's growing awareness of how very precisely and sensitively Katsumi understands her voice and her music.

Once again, such dialogue as there is between them has to occur through the medium of Gen, Hosokawa's interpreter. In light of this, it's meaningful that Gen has fallen in love with the young rebel Carmen, and you'll have read their dialogue in scenes where he's teaching her how to read and write in Spanish and English, scenes of growing attraction and love-making.

Finally, towards the end of the novel, Hosokawa, at Roxanne's invitation, has spent the night with her in her bedroom. The narrative leaves you at the door, and you next read of them together late on the following morning; just after Roxanne's excited intervention into a young male guard's singing has given him the mistaken impression that the great opera singer didn't like it. Roxanne and Katsume are among all the others in the reception room.

'I shouldn't have told him to stop,' Roxanne said. Gen translated it into Japanese.

'There is no place for the boy to go,' Mr. Hokosawa said. 'He will have to come back. You mustn't worry about that.' In Japan, he was often made uneasy by this modern age of affection, young men and women holding hands in public, kissing good-bye on subway trains. There was nothing about these gestures he had understood. He had believed that what a man felt in his heart was a private matter and so should remain with him, but he had never had so much in his heart before. There wasn't enough room for this much love and it left an aching sensation in his chest. Heartache! Who would have thought it was true? Now all he wanted was to take her hand or curve his arm around her shoulder.

Roxanne Coss leaned towards him, dipped her head down to his shoulder just for a second, just long enough for her cheek to touch his shirt.

'Ah,' said Mr Hosokawa softly, 'You are everything in the world to me.'

Gen looked at him. Was that meant to be translated, the tenderness his employer whispered? Mr Hokosawa took one of Roxanne's hands. He held it up to his chest, touched it to his shirt in the place above his heart. He nodded. Was he nodding to Gen? Was he telling Gen to go ahead? Or was he nodding to her? Gen felt a terrible discomfort. He wanted to turn away. It was a private matter. He knew what that meant now.

'Everything in the world,' Mr Hokosawa said again, but this time he looked at Gen.

And so Gen told her. He tried to make his voice soft. 'Respectfully,' he said to Roxanne, 'Mr Hokosawa would like you to know that you are everything in the world to him.' He remembered saying something similar to her from the Russian.

It was to her credit that Roxanne never looked at Gen. She kept her eyes exactly on Mr Hosokawa's eyes and took the words from him.

This is a dialogue scene with very little dialogue, but every word of dialogue is worked by the narrative to create the intense effect of romance, not the least of which is its very public setting.

Write two scenes of dialogue

Write two 500-word scenes of dialogue. In the first, the dialogue should predominate over the narrative by a ratio of at least eight to one (8:1). In the second scene, the narrative should dominate the dialogue by the same ratio. In both, of course, the narrative should inform the dialogue, and both scenes should develop the characters.

Loading dialogue with context to develop character

Iain Banks's novel *The Quarry* (2013) is narrated by 18-year-old Kit. He lives with his father Guy in a big old dilapidated house backing on to a deep quarry. Guy is dying. Kit is very intelligent but socially inept. He's autistic.

In contemporary fiction, the autistic character (in the mild to middle range of autism) has replaced the nineteenth- and twentieth-century holy fool, or idiot savant (also called the wise fool), probably because scientific knowledge has replaced religious and mystical belief, but the character continues on as a moral touchstone, a sort of absolute of objectivity in an otherwise subjective fictive world. The distinctions between wise fool and autistic character are intellectual as well as social. The autistic character has a super-rational scientific or mathematical mind; the wise fool is generally without formal education but is intuitive and psychologically astute. The autistic character notices, in fine detail, special relationships, clothing, mannerisms and, often indirectly, the facial and bodily expressions of others. The wise fool looks past external details directly into the 'soul' of others and feels their feelings.

The Quarry's action takes place over a holiday weekend at Kit and Guy's house when a group of Guy's old friends come for one last time to visit the dying man who was once their film-making teacher at university. As Kit welcomes Holly, the first to arrive and the closest to Guy and Kit, the scene opens; its structure is typical of dialogue scenes in the novel.

I open the door. 'Holly!'

'Kit,' she says and comes forward and hugs me, kissing me on both sides of the face. She rises on tiptoes to do this, and properly applies lip pressure to my cheeks, a couple of centimetres forward from each of my ears. There is no moisture transferred (thankfully, even if it is Hol), but it is more than the usual mwah-mwah that I know, through Hol, media people exchange, when there may be no physical contact between heads at all, just cheeks put briefly in proximity.

Hol's hair looks the same so I don't have to remember to compliment her on this, and she appears similar otherwise, which is good. She is dressed in blue jeans, a black T-shirt and a green fleece. It is mostly thanks to Hol – and a little due to Mrs Willoughby – that I know to look for those things and consider commenting on them, to keep people happy.

'How are you, love?' she asks me.

I like the way Hol says 'love'. She was brought up near Bolton but her accent is sort of placeless; if you were forced to, you might say she sounded vaguely like a Londoner – or at least somebody from the Home Counties – with a hint of American. Dad says she completely lost what he calls her 'Ay-oop' accent within the first year of uni, remaking herself to sound less provincial, less identifiable, more neutral and bland. But she still says 'love' like a northerner, with the vowel sound like the one in 'low', not the one in 'above'. I realize I am thinking about this rather than actually replying to her question when I notice that there's an ongoing silence and Hol is looking at me with both eyebrows raised.

'Oh,' I say. 'Generally pretty well, thanks.'

'Huh,' Mrs Gunn says, appearing silently, suddenly at my side. Mrs Gunn is small, wiry, seemingly always bent over – forwards – and wears what we're all pretty sure is a tightly curled auburn wig. 'It's you,' she says to Hol. She turns away again, heading back down the dark hall, drying her hands violently on a dishcloth. 'I suppose you'd better come in,' she says as she goes.

'Nice to see you too, Mrs G,' Hol says quietly to our housekeeper's retreating back. She puts a small rucksack into my arms.

'Oh,' I say, startled, looking at it. 'I haven't got you anything.'

Hol sighs, takes the rucksack back. 'Never mind. I'll take this; you can get my case from the car. Heavier anyway.'

She stands aside and I go out to the car – the same old Polo – and take her case from the hatch. The car is red – the paint is faded on the short bonnet, which I've noticed tends to happen with red cars – and its rear is grey with motorway grime, making the hatch release feel gritty. I wipe my hand on my trousers but I'll need to wash it again as soon as I can. Or I could just stand here with my arm outstretched and my hand flat like I was looking for a tip from God; it is, as usual, raining.

'How's Guy?' Hol asks as we go up the stairs to her old room.

'Oh, still dying,' I tell her.

'Jeez, Kit,' she mutters, and I see her looking along the dark corridor towards his room.

I open the door for her and bring her case in as she stands there, looking across the rucked carpet and the sagging bed to the window with the faded curtains and the view over the densely treed back garden. The trees are only now coming into bud, so you can see the quarry between the network of restlessly moving twigs and branches, a grey depth opening into the rainy distance.

'Was I being insensitive?' I ask her.

What the dialogue looks like here isn't much like scenes of dialogue in most other books. Kit, the narrator, wants to reply to his father and his friend Hol, but he has to process the information he hears very consciously, so that he gives the proper, that is, emotionally considerate, reply. The emotional intelligence he lacks he tries to make up for (you note he's being taught about this by Hol and a Mrs Willoughby) with his intellectual intelligence and excellent memory. But this takes time. Meanwhile, Hol waits a bit impatiently for his reply. You, the reader, don't because his thought process is original and interesting. He's trying to get along in a verbal world that mixes connotation with denotation, metaphor and irony. But his mindset is almost hard-wired to be literal, so sometimes his logic is very wrong, sometimes funny, and sometimes full of odd-angle insight. The author has to remind you that the other character is waiting for an answer, because you're content to keep listening to what can be considered Kit's internal monologue – a special sort of dialogue.

There are other aspects of Kit's narration linked to his autism. At the start of the excerpt above, rather than saying of Hol after he greets her with 'Holly!' something direct like 'She hugs me', he says she 'comes forward and hugs me', making a point that a non-autistic person would take for granted – that in order to hug him, she has to move her body closer to his. Anxiety about crowds and an aversion to physical closeness with another body are not uncommon in autism. His description of Hol kissing his cheeks is enormously detailed, scientific, and strange for it: 'kissing me on both sides of the face'; 'properly applies lip pressure to my cheeks, a couple of centimetres forward from each of my ears'. The most unexpected word here is 'properly', a reminder to himself that he has learned this way of kissing is all right. In this context the word is touching. He's trying hard to put up with this. When he tells you 'There is no moisture transferred (thankfully, even if it is Hol)', you know that this is the dislike of physical contact, of another's secretions, that characterizes some autism. From this point, Kit moves on to contrast this real kissing of friendship with the social 'mwah-mwah' kissing that makes no contact. This shows that he does understand the difference that Hol's explained about how media people greet. Again, Kit likes Hol very much so he tries to put up with a form of contact that he knows will please Hol more than mwah-mwah make-believe.

Note how Banks loads this opening narrative in the novel's first non-flashback scene with a range of 'autistic' elements so that you quickly learn to identify those of Kit's responses that are outside the ordinary. The first-person narration has the advantage of creating a more vividly dramatic exposition of these important aspects of Kit's character.

In the same way, the next paragraph's opening: 'Hol's hair looks the same so I don't have to remember to compliment her on this', shows how consciously Kit has to work at being 'normally' social. Kit's artless admission that 'It is mostly thanks to Hol – and a little due to Mrs Willoughby [a specialist teacher] – that I know to look for those things and consider commenting on them, to keep people happy.' His literal explanation is itself a mark of his autism that attracts us to his character: he tries and tries.

Kit then reflects on Hol's accent when she calls him 'love'. It's the northern sound of it he so likes. In this paragraph you can make out entire thoughts, perhaps verbatim, remembered from his father's talk about Hol's accent. That Kit's debt to his nurture is so clearly expressed within the structure (stricture) of his nature is another curiously touching phenomenon of his character. He will reveal himself to you because he can do no other.

At this point in his inner discourse on accents, he realizes 'that there's an ongoing silence and Hol is looking at me with both eyebrows raised', so he finally answers her question 'How are you, love?' ('with the vowel sound like the one in "low", not the one in "above"').

He works so hard at thinking of social context that it produces funny mistakes. When Hol suddenly hands him her rucksack to take up to her room, he thinks of what he's been told about the importance of reciprocity in friendship and his response is '"Oh," I say, startled, "I haven't got you anything."'

Most starkly revealing of his problems with emotion is Kit's response to Hol asking 'How's Guy?' He says, 'Oh, still dying.' She replies with a muttered 'Jeez, Kit', voicing your own slight shock of what in other people you'd take for callousness, even viciousness. It's only when, after helping take her luggage up to her room and watching Hol stare out of its window for a while with her back to him, that you get his 'Was I being insensitive?'. This is affecting, this use of his high sensual and intellectual intelligence to try to compensate for his low emotional understanding.

When Hol hugs him and tells him he smells a bit, he relates the physical proximity as he naturally would, with an autistic's exactness. He's just thought hard of what he should say or do in this position – or allow Hol to do – to make her feel she's comforting him and so feel better herself. After she comments on his smell, he notes: 'though she doesn't lift her head away from where it is, her nose near my left armpit. She briefly squeezes me a little tighter, as though to compensate for the personal criticism.' Artless, yes, but intelligent, too, learning about the emotions of others.

All of his physical repulsion and work to overcome it at the relatively casual level may be charming and even amusing, but in this same first chapter of the novel you very soon come to a scene showing Kit working to cope at a more intense and powerful level.

'Is there blood?'

'There is a little blood.'

'Well, what does that mean? What does "a little" mean?'

'It means there is a little blood.'

'Don't be fucking smart, Kit; just tell me how much blood there is. And what colour? Red? Brown? Black?'

'Are you sure you can't turn round and take a look?'

'Not without going out into the fucking hall, waddling, with my trousers around my ankles and my cock hanging out, so, no.'

'If I had a smartphone I could take a photo and show you.'

'I'm not buying you a fucking smartphone. Will you shut up about the fucking smartphone? You don't need one. And you'll just post the photos on Facebook. Or find a way to sell them in your stupid game.'

'Course I wouldn't,' I tell him. 'Though you could have Faecesbook, I suppose,' I add. Well, you have to try to lighten the mood.

'Oh, Christ.'

'There's only a smear,' I tell him. 'And it's red.'

'Good, fine. Look, just, just, you know, wipe me off and… Christ, this is… Just, would you? Okay?'

This doesn't happen all the time but, sometimes, I have to wipe my dad clean after he's moved his bowels. He can't stretch round or underneath any more to do it himself; even on the opiates the pain is too much now that the cancer has moved into his spine. Often Mrs Gunn will do this. She's paid to be a carer now, though I'm not sure this whole arse-cleaning thing is really within her remit. Guy cried following the first time she performed this service for him. He doesn't know that I know this; I heard him through his bedroom door afterwards.

The first time I had to help Guy wipe himself I tried to do it with my eyes closed. This was unsuccessful, and messy. My compromise these days is to breathe through my mouth so I don't smell whatever might be in the toilet bowl

(I resent being made to look in there but Guy feels a need to know whether there is blood in his stool). Obviously I am wearing a pair of surgical gloves; we keep a box by the door. I can let myself into the downstairs loo because it has a relatively modern mechanism that can be unlocked from outside via a slot in a small metal stub projecting beneath the handle. You use a screwdriver, or a penny.

[...]

After half a minute or so he stops coughing and goes back to just wheezing.

'That you okay?' I ask him.

'Fucking never been better,' he says. He hauls some phlegm up into his mouth, shuffles back a little further on the loo, and carefully spits between his spread legs. I choose not to follow the whole process. 'Christ,' he says, sitting back against the cistern and breathing hard, a noise of gurgling coming from his lungs, 'Knackers me just having a cough these days.' He sighs, wipes his lips, looks at me. 'I hope the shareholders of British American Tobacco are fucking grateful.'

'Think we're done?' I ask him.

'Done and dusted, kid,' he tells me. 'Done and dust-to-dusted.'

I flush a second time, strip off the gloves and dump them in the bin, help Guy on with his pants and trousers and run the taps, holding the towel ready while he rests his forearms on the Zimmer and washes his hands.

'Okay, okay,' he says. 'I'm all right. Stop fussing.'

I don't think I was fussing but I've learned there's no point arguing. I head back to the sitting room and hear him lock the loo door. He doesn't like me to accompany him back into the room when we have guests, so making it obvious he needs help in the toilet. There are still proprieties – or at least little face-saving deceptions – you can observe even when you're reduced to this level of helplessness.

And, of course, it's only going to get worse, as we both know.

Here are the conditions – the limits, phobias maybe – already established about Kit when you come to read this scene: he doesn't like to be in close confinement with anyone else; he's hyper-sensitive to dirt of any sort on his skin or near him; he's rational and logical to a fault; he cannot, as a result, really lie; he dislikes swearing, perhaps because it is connected in his mind with the first two conditions, since much swearing is denotatively sexual.

When you read this scene you tend to experience it through identification with its narrator, Kit, yet you're also sympathetic to the physical and psychological suffering of his father. The scene opens with Kit, whose ability to note anything he observes is usually so objective, not shying away from observation. He's asked to look carefully into the toilet bowl at his father's faeces. Kit's intellect is stymied by his repulsion. He prevaricates: to Guy's 'What does "a little" mean?' he replies, 'It means there is a little blood.' Guy, in anguish, has no patience; his rejoinder contains much swearing and demands that Kit describe both the amount of blood and the colour of the blood in his stool. But Kit can't yet bring himself to look so closely and asks whether Guy's certain that he can't turn around to look. Note that to this point there has been no explicit reference to where this scene is taking place. Guy's answer provides one. 'Not without going into the fucking hall, waddling, with my trousers round my ankles and my cock hanging out, so, no.'

This reply is both self-lacerating and self-pitying, yet it's difficult for you to reject this self-pity. The reply is also particularly hard on Kit, who Guy must know, as you do, has special dislike of both its content and its diction; Guy's ending his reasons with 'and my cock hanging out' is especially repulsive, even abusive.

Kit continues to stall, suggesting that if Guy bought him a smartphone he could just take a photo of the toilet bowl and show it to him. This is an 18-year-old's ploy, but it actually would be less difficult for Kit to point the phone rather than his face at the toilet. Guy loses all patience at this, implying that it's a constant wheedling request for a merely expensive, fashionable gadget, one that might have Kit posting photos of Guy's stool on Facebook. Kit answers, '"Course I wouldn't," I tell him. "Though you could have Faecesbook, I suppose," I add. Well, you have to try to lighten the mood.' But, finally, there are no more diversions, and Kit reports '"There's only a smear," I tell him. "And it's red."'

What's happening is that you're continuously attracted and repelled in this scene, understanding the father's demands, understanding the son's reluctance. Banks has structured the scene so that its catharsis (the tension between attraction and repulsion, pity and fear) is both figurative as it relates to literary theory and, of course, awfully literal. Why doubt that Banks was very aware of the wordplay behind this bowel-moving scene? The point is that this is powerful development of character in dialogue as well as descriptive narrative.

Another point worth mentioning is that Kit's rational, observant character can make you feel emotion, even though its presentation with Kit as narrator is naturally objective. First, look at Kit relating his father's rejection of his offers to look after Guy's mobile phone and its charger and his medications: 'but he just accuses me of trying to run his life and tells me to back off.' You're pretty certain that Guy has used the word 'off', but you're also pretty certain that the word before it was not 'back'. There is something here in Kit's de-vulgarizing his father's language that's touching and sweet, despite its source in a phobia that is neither moral nor sentimental, as if you suspend your own knowledge of the character's limitations, as if you were made to emotionalize and humanize the autistic teenager.

Next come these rational observations: 'Guy stands, bending forward to rest on the Zimmer frame. I flush the toilet, to be rid of the sight, then while his always skinny, now scrawny, legs quiver, I carefully wipe him down.' These details on his legs are as full of care as his 'carefully' wiping his father. If this isn't the care of real love, you feel it's as good as.

Despite the scene's repulsive elements – or perhaps because of them – it's full of humour: light, dark and darker. There's Kit's response about his photo of his father's stool getting on to Facebook when he says, 'Course I wouldn't... Though you could have Faecesbook, I suppose.' This isn't hugely funny, but as Kit says, it's an attempt 'to lighten the mood'. But after he wipes Guy, he tells you, 'Once you get over the simple unpleasantness of it ... it is easier to wipe somebody else's bum than it is your own, because you can see what you're doing and use both hands at once if necessary. The whole process is much more efficient and uses no more toilet paper than is strictly required, so it's better for the environment, too. If we were really being green we'd all have somebody else wipe our bums, though I don't see it catching on.' This is really funny, Kit's logical mind going on until it reaches its *reductio ad absurdum*.

After Guy's horrible coughing fit, the result, like his sickness, of his smoking, he wheezes, 'I hope the shareholders of British American Tobacco are fucking grateful.' This is very dark. And in response to Kit's 'Think we're done?' Guy's 'Done and dusted, kid... Done and dust-to dusted' is darker still, a sick joke.

In the above discussions of dialogue in *The Quarry*, much space has been spent looking closely at the descriptive narrative of Kit, at his commentary. It's necessary in order to understand how the narrative 'loads' the dialogue with specific context, and how that dialogue subsequently develops character.

If you look back over this chapter, you'll find you've been through a fairly wide – though obviously nowhere inclusive – range of how different ways of presenting dialogue work to develop character in depth.

Write a scene with two characters

Write a 750-word scene involving two characters. One is in the position of being dependent on the other. The other (child, spouse, partner or friend) loves or is fond of the character dependent on her or him, but suffers from the sometimes rough treatment or language of the 'caregetter'. The scene should be one in which dialogue dominates. If you can get humour into it, despite the scene's potential grimness, so much the better.

Workshop

This workshop differs from earlier ones in asking you to produce the start of a piece of fiction for which some research will probably be required. The piece, of around 750 to 1,000 words, is to be a scene of dialogue between two or three people who know each other.

One of the characters, at least as important if not more important than the others, doesn't act and speak like the other(s). (This does *not* mean a lisp, stutter or other speech impediment.) She or he might be deaf, autistic or have some nervous or mental disorder that sets particular limitations and/ or characteristics on his or her speech. The idea is to use what you know or find by research about this condition to make the character interesting – *not* as a clinical case study but as a living person in her/his relation to the other(s) through what she or he says.

Focus points

- Dialogue is a naturally powerful way of showing character.
- Not only can dialogue format vary greatly but the proportion of dialogue in any two pieces of fiction may be wildly different.
- The language used in dialogue can employ subtle differences in diction to convey important information about character. Shifts in tone and formality of speech can express different characters' social background, mood and intention.
- Dialogue scenes may contain at least as much descriptive narrative and narration of inner thought and feeling as dialogue itself. Alternatively, the bulk of the narrative may be presented before and after the dialogue.
- First-person narration and internal monologue – a special sort of dialogue – enable a character to reveal his or her own qualities as well as aspects of the other characters.
- Using a 'wise fool' character is an effective way of looking past external details directly into the feelings of others.

Next step

The next chapter studies characters developed using symbols and satire.

7

Character: symbolism and satire

The use of symbolism is an important way of revealing character and is often used to show the reader things about a character that the character himself is unaware of. Using symbolism to develop character in fiction is certainly more widespread than the development of a symbolic character. However, symbolic characters occur much more often in fiction than symbolic structures such as parable or – rarest of all today – allegory.

Satire in fiction may be general or specific. General satire is often characterized by a series of increasingly improbable incidents throughout the story, building up to a climax. Specific satire takes aim at a particular character type and is often conducted through the narrative voice as well as through dialogue. Fictional satire has many formal means of presentation.

The use of symbolism

Looking back to Chapter 3's discussion of Claire Messud's novel *The Woman Upstairs*, you find an example of symbolism used to develop the central character Nora, the narrator. The art she makes is symbolic; that is, it's real but it's also representative of her character. Nora, you'll recall, makes extremely small, intensely detailed replicas of the rooms of historical women artists to whom she's drawn. These finely crafted rooms are so small that they can be viewed and appreciated by only one person at a time. Very few people have ever seen her art, and those few have been personally invited to do so by Nora because she's judged them trustworthy. She believes them sensitive enough to respond in the ways she intends, to experience these rooms' levels of meaning, commentary and compassion with the particular woman artist – as Nora does herself.

In other words, Nora makes sure that anyone who sees her art will like it.

In contrast, her artist friend Sirena, with whom she shares a studio, creates an opposite sort of art: vast installations which many people at once can experience, can walk within and interact with, reacting as they will. This creates another symbolic rendering of Nora's art and nature in direct opposition.

Nora begins and ends the novel by warning you to watch out; she's angry and she's going to show the world! In fact, the novel shows you otherwise. Nora is not really an artist inasmuch as she refuses to put her art out there to any real audience. You may like her (ex) friend Sirena's art or not like it, but Sirena is an artist because she sets out what she makes for anyone and everyone to make of it what they will – good, bad, ugly or nothing at all. Nora is too circumspect, too frightened to understand this.

 Key idea

Symbolism can be used to let the reader understand what characters cannot understand about themselves.

The use of allegory and parable

On the whole, full, rounded character development is difficult in allegory, where one-to-one equivalence between major elements in the storyline and generalized symbolic meanings typically demands a flattening of character. Put conversely, character individuation tends to obscure generalized symbolic meaning, such characters tending to represent only themselves rather than 'mankind' or people of 'developed western nations' or 'contemporary Americans'. Examples of such necessary flatness of character can be found in Shirley Jackson's well-known story 'The Lottery' and in E.M. Forster's less well-known story 'The Other Side of the Hedge', the former an allegory of obedience to convention and superstition, the latter an allegory of the closeness of death 'even in the midst of life'. Allegory shouldn't be confused for novels with a general, less exact symbolic meaning, such as William Golding's *Lord of the Flies* or *The Spire*. These could be considered parables.

Parable offers more scope for character development since it has less of a one-to-one specific symbolic equivalence than an overall representation of a particular moral, social or historical meaning which the writer usually maintains as a truth. So, in Tolstoy's short story 'How Much Land Does a Man Require?', much distinctive detail can be given to the character's nature and behaviour as he quests for more land, just as long as the final action and outcome occur – in other words, just as long as the plot mechanism results in the particular climax and denouement needed to make the moral point about need and greed.

Parable in fiction is also possible through a character being developed symbolically so that what he or she is – and how this affects and represents the overall story – suggests a broadly parallel meaning without the precise equivalence of allegory.

Symbolic character development

One contemporary example of such symbolic character development is in Cormac McCarthy's novel **Blood Meridian** (1985). The novel is loosely based on the historical Glanton gang, mercenary marauders along both sides of the US–Mexican border during the years 1849–50, years during which the mythic 'West' was being 'won'. The novel follows the life of a 16-year-old runaway referred to only as 'the kid'. The kid, Glanton, and all the other major characters – but for one – are presented within the conventions of realism. The one who isn't is named Holden, but is mostly called 'the judge'.

Here is the scene of his first appearance, in the novel's first chapter:

The Reverend Green had been playing to a full house daily as long as the rain had been falling and the rain had been falling for two weeks. When the kid ducked into the ratty canvas tent there was standing room along the walls, a place or two, and such a heady reek of the wet and bathless that they themselves would sally forth into the downpour now and again for fresh air before the rain drove them in again. He stood with others of his kind along the back wall. The only thing that might have distinguished him in that crowd was that he was not armed.

Neighbors, said the reverend, he couldnt stay out of these here hell, hell, hellholes right here in Nacogdoches. I said to him, said: You goin to take the Son of God in there with ye? And he said: Oh no. No I aint. And I said: Don't you know that he said I will foller ye always even unto the end of the road?

Well, he said, I aint askin nobody to go nowhere. And I said: Neighbor, you dont need to ask. He's a goin to be there with ye ever step of the way whether ye ask it or ye don't. I said: Neighbor, you caint get shed of him. Are you going to drag him, him, into that hellhole yonder?

You ever see such a place for rains?

The kid had been watching the reverend. He turned to the man who spoke. He wore a long moustache after the fashion of teamsters and he wore a widebrim hat with a low round crown. He was slightly walleyed and he was watching the kid earnestly as if he'd know his opinion about the rain,

I just got here, said the kid.

Well it beats all I ever seen.

The kid nodded. An enormous man dressed in an oilcloth slicker had entered the tent and removed his hat. He was bald as a stone and had no trace of beard and he had no brows to his eyes nor lashes to them. He was close to seven feet in height and he stood smoking a cigar even in this nomadic house of God and he seemed to have removed his hat only to chase the rain from it for now he put it on again.

The reverend had stopped his sermon altogether. There was no sound in the tent. All watched the man. He adjusted the hat and then pushed his way forward as far as the crateboard pulpit where the reverend stood and there he turned to address the reverend's congregation. His face was serene and strangely childlike. His hands were small. He held them out.

Ladies and gentlemen I feel it my duty to inform you that the man holding this revival is an imposter. He holds no papers of divinity from any institution recognized or improvised. He is altogether devoid of the least qualification to the office he has usurped and has only committed to memory a few passages from the good book for the purpose of lending to his fraudulent sermons some faint flavour of the piety he despises. In truth, the gentleman standing here before you passing as a minister of the Lord is not only totally illiterate but is also wanted by the law in the states of Tennessee, Kentucky, Mississippi, and Arkansas.

Oh God, cried the reverend. Lies, lies! He began reading feverishly from his opened bible.

On a variety of charges the most recent of which involved a girl of eleven years – I said eleven – who had come to him in trust and whom he was surprised in the act of violating while actually clothed in the livery of God.

A moan swept through the crowd. A lady sank to her knees.

This is him, cried the reverend, sobbing. This is him. The devil. Here he stands.

Let's hang the turd, called an ugly thug from the gallery to the rear.

Not three weeks before this he was run out of Fort Smith Arkansas for having congress with a goat. Yes lady, that is what I said. Goat.

Why damn my eyes if I wont shoot the son of a bitch, said a man rising at the far side of the tent, and drawing a pistol from his boot he levelled it and fired. The young teamster instantly produced a knife from his clothing and unseamed the tent and stepped outside into the rain. The kid followed. They ducked low and ran across the mud toward the hotel. Already gunfire was general within the tent and a dozen exits had been hacked through the canvas walls and people were pouring out, women screaming, folk stumbling, folk trampled underfoot in the mud. The kid and his friend reached the hotel gallery and wiped the water from their eyes and turned to watch. As they did so the tent began to sway and buckle and like a huge and wounded medusa it slowly settled to the ground trailing tattered canvas walls and ratty guyropes over the ground.

The baldheaded man was already at the bar when they entered. On the polished wood before him were two hats and a double handful of coins.

He raised his glass but not to them. They stood up to the bar and ordered whiskeys and the kid laid his money down but the barman pushed it back with his thumb and nodded.

This here is on the judge, he said.

They drank. The teamster set his glass down and looked at the kid or he seemed to, you couldn't be sure of his gaze. The kid looked down the bar to where the judge stood. The bar was that tall not every man could even get his elbows up on it but it came just to the judge's waist and he stood with his hands placed flatwise on the wood, leaning slightly, as if about to give another address. By now men were piling through the doorway, bleeding, covered in mud, cursing. They gathered about the judge. A posse was being drawn to pursue the preacher.

Judge, how did you come to have the goods on that no account?

Goods? Said the judge.

When was you in Fort Smith?

Fort Smith?

Where did you know him to know all that stuff on him?

You mean the Reverend Green?

Yessir. I reckon you was in Fort Smith fore ye came out here.

I was never in Fort Smith in my life. Doubt that he was.

They looked from one to the other.

Well where was it you run up on him?

I never laid eyes on the man before today. Never even heard of him.

He raised his glass and drank.

There was a strange silence in the room. The men looked like mud effigies. Finally someone began to laugh. Then another. Soon they were all laughing together. Someone bought the judge a drink.

In its form, this is very like a Mark Twain scene of the same period, but in Twain it would be the bad guy, the con man, the judge, who would be run out of town. Here, a posse forms to catch the reverend and no doubt shoot or hang him. The opening words of this scene, however, suggest an entertainment, with 'The Reverend had been playing to a full house daily' also suggesting that he's only playing, only acting the role, and this is associated with an audience that partly wishes merely to be entertained, and also that the preacher is trying to dupe money from the congregation. But this is no parody sermon. And there's no mention of a plea for money.

And such is the nature of the half-bored crowd that when the 'enormous man' enters, all eyes are on him and the reverend stops preaching. Indeed, the judge is something to look at: almost seven feet tall, absolutely hairless, no eyebrows, no eyelashes, and smoking in church.

When the big man pushes up to the pulpit and begins his denunciation of the reverend, he speaks in a highly educated and articulate voice, challenging the preacher's qualifications and going on to say he's 'totally illiterate'. Although McCarthy immediately writes that the judge's interjection has the reverend 'reading feverishly from the opened bible', no one in the crowd notices this under the magnetism of the judge's own sermon on the evil of the preacher. He tells the crowd the preacher is wanted by the law in several states, and as his victim denies this, the judge talks over him, listing horrid deeds – the violation of an 11-year-old girl, sexual congress with a goat, such lurid crimes that no one pays attention to the reverend calling to them through his sobs that 'This is him. The devil. Here he stands.'

This isn't at all Mark Twain's jovial irony. The lying judge triumphs – someone fires a gun at the reverend, others start shooting, the crowd cuts its way out through the canvas walls and people are trampled in the mud. The next image of the judge is him standing at the hotel bar buying everyone drinks from the coins taken from two hats. McCormac never describes the judge stealing the collection in the melee. As if by magic, the gigantic figure disappears from one scene he's created and appears in a different location to create another scene. As he's questioned by the crowd who've come from the tent, he questions them back until he says he's never laid eyes on the reverend before nor ever heard of him. That the men are for a moment dumbstruck is curiously modified by the next sentence: 'The men looked like mud effigies.' This 'strange silence' is the moment of moral challenge, but not one of the men is up to it: they are like mud, like clay in the judge's hand. One man responds with a laugh; soon they're all laughing, delighted with this cruelty. The scene ends with 'Someone bought the judge a drink.' It's powerful and chilling. At this point, though you may sense there's something strange, very strange, about the man, I think you don't quite accept him as something essentially inhuman, unhuman. But McCarthy has only begun to develop this peculiar character.

The judge isn't present when the kid meets up with and joins a troop of Americans under a Captain White, a man who wants to keep fighting the Mexicans even after the United States has signed a peace treaty with Mexico. The scene of the kid's recruitment reveals the political and social culture in which the judge flourishes. The dialogue – speeches – following are part of the captain's recruitment talk.

The captain leaned back and folded his arms. What we are
dealing with, he said, is a race of degenerates little better
than niggers. And maybe no better. There is no government
in Mexico. Hell, there is no God in Mexico. Never will

be. We are dealing with a people manifestly incapable of
governing themselves. And do you know what happens
with people who cannot govern themselves? That's right.
Others come in to govern for them.

[...]

The captain was watching the kid. The kid looked uneasy.
Son, said the captain. We are to be the instruments of
liberation in a dark and troubled land. That's right. We are
to spearhead the drive.

[...]

He leaned forward and placed his hands on his knees.
And we will be the ones who will divide the spoils. There
will be a section of land for every man in my company.
Fine grassland. Some of the finest in the world. A land
rich in minerals, in gold and silver I would say beyond the
wildest speculation.

Here, the politics of exceptionalism comes with its typical mixture of racism, anarchy and colonial aspiration. The Mexicans need a superior people to govern them because they're 'a race of degenerates little better than niggers'. The captain says there is neither government nor God in Mexico. He says they are dealing with 'a people *manifestly* [my emphasis] incapable of governing themselves'. McCarthy gives the captain this particular adverb to call to mind the concept of 'manifest destiny', that loose collection of special reasons and beliefs around in the United States during the first half of the nineteenth century, among which was the idea that it was America's destiny to extend from the Atlantic to the Pacific, to bring its superior way of government and way of life, including religion, to less enlightened peoples and countries; in other words, what the British were later to call 'the white man's burden' in justifying their imperial, colonial takeovers.

The anarchy engendered by such an attitude is an important force in the social–moral atmosphere of the novel, a space in which the judge can operate with some impunity, whether he's human or not. And whatever he is, it's not a stock Old West character. For one thing, he's hugely knowledgeable. Here he is on geology and, from geology, on evolution.

In the afternoon he sat in the compound breaking ore
samples with a hammer, the fieldspar rich in red oxide of
copper and native nuggets in whose organic lobations he
purported to read news of the earth's origins, holding an

extemporary lecture in geology to a small gathering who
nodded and spat. A few would quote him scripture to
confound his ordering up of eons out of the ancient chaos
and other apostate supposing. The judge smiled.

Books lie, he said.

God don't lie.

No, said the judge. He does not. And these are his words.

He held up a chunk of rock.

He speaks in stones and trees, the bones of things.

The squatters in their rags nodded among themselves and
were soon reckoning him correct, this man of learning, in
all his speculations, and this the judge encouraged until
they were right proselytes of the new order whereupon he
laughed at them for fools.

Like Darwin or other early evolutionists, the judge is able to integrate God into his scientific understanding. But he can't really be satisfied with so easy a conversion to reason of this bunch of rag-tag adventurers before him, so he cynically scorns them for their weak-mindedness.

The judge's knowledge is practical as well as theoretical. The judge, now riding with Glanton's gang, to which to kid belongs, is being discussed by Tobin, another gang member, also known as the expriest. He says to the kid, 'the man's a hand at anything. I've never seen him turn to a task but what he didn't prove clever at it'. When the kid says he's seen the judge before, in Nacogdoches, Tobin says, 'Every man in the company claims to have encountered that sootysouled rascal in some other place.' Then he says, 'He saved us all, I have to give him that,' and he proceeds to tell the kid the story of how they left Chihuahua City a band of 38 men and were down to 14, without any gunpowder left, being followed by a large band of Apaches bent to kill them all. Then the judge turned up. Just like that, they came upon him as if he'd just materialized, sitting on a rock in the middle of the desert, no horse, just a canvas kit bag and an old blanket over his shoulder, and a rifle mounted in silver with its name in silver wire: *Et in Arcadia ego*, which the expriest knows means something about death in the midst of life. The judge didn't even have water, just waiting as if he knew they'd show up. He immediately made friends with Glanton – the expriest calls it a 'horrible covenant' – and became a sort of co-leader.

The judge then led the gang up into the mountains, picking leaves from trees and bushes as he rode and pressing them into a notebook. He led them to a cave, not for shelter but to collect the bat guano. He then leached out the guano with creek water and wood ash. Then he built a clay kiln and started burning charcoal in it and after a few days came up with 'eight pounds of pure saltpetre and about three pounds of fine alder charcoal'. Then, the Apaches getting closer, the judge led them across the badlands and up to the crater of an old volcano where he chipped away at the brimstone, had the others join in, and they collected it and chopped it fine with their knives, as the judge directed. Then, after dumping out the charcoal and nitre, the judge poured in the sulphur. But since there was no water, he asked everyone to follow him in pissing into the mixture.

By now, the Apaches were climbing the volcano. The judge kneaded the mixture to a paste and spread it thin with a knife, as did the others following him, to dry in the sun. He told the men to scrape it off and grind it to a powder, to gunpowder. He then tested it out into the crater and it worked. Then he poured it into each man's powder horn and flask, and they did this 'circlin past him like communicants'. The judge then went to the edge and in full view of the Apaches stood and waved a white shirt and shouted to them in Spanish that all were dead except him and asked them to have mercy on him. The expriest says, 'God it sent them yappin on the slope like dogs and he turns to us, the judge, with that smile of his, and he says: Gentlemen. That was all he said.' Then the judge started to fire on the Apaches with a pistol in each hand because, as the expriest puts it, he's 'eitherhanded as a spider, he can write with both hands at a time and I've seen him do it, and he commenced to kill Indians. We needed no second invitation. God it was butchery.' He tells the kid this was his first experience of the judge. The kid then asks:

> What's he a judge of?
> What's he a judge of.
> Tobin glanced off across the fire. Ah lad, he said. Hush now. The man will hear you. He has ears like a fox.

Engineer as well as scientist, technician as well as theorist, the judge is American know-how and ingenuity, and its end is murder. The expriest Tobin's story is itself a parable of the devil, but McCarthy has more to offer as symbolic suggestion. When Tobin and the judge sit talking about vanished people like the Anasazi of the Southwest,

Tobin asks how children should be raised so that mankind can improve through its generations. The judge responds:

If God meant to interfere in the degeneracy of mankind would he have not done so by now? Wolves cull themselves, man. What other creature could? And is the race of man not more predacious yet? The way of the world is to bloom and to flower and die but in the affairs of men there is no waning and the noon of his expression signals the onset of night. His spirit is exhausted at the peak of its achievement. His meridian is at once his darkening and the evening of his day. He loves games? Let him play for stakes. This you see here, these [Anasazi] ruins wondered at by tribes of savages, do you not think that this will be again? Aye. And again. With other people, with other sons.

The judge looked about him. He was sat before the fire naked save for his breeches and his hands rested palm down upon his knees. His eyes were empty slots. None among the company harboured any notion as to what this attitude implied, yet so like an icon was he in his sitting that they grew cautious and spoke with circumspection among themselves as if they would not waken something that had better been left sleeping.

If all this weren't suggestive enough of the judge as that which knows yet denies, derides, and destroys, McCarthy gives you the judge in an unmistakable, unforgettable image.

Each dawn as they saddled their horses they watched the pale mountains to the north and to the west for any trace of smoke. There was none. The scouts would be already gone, riding out in the dark before the sun rose, and they would not return until night, reckoning out the camp in that incoordinate waste by palest starlight or in blackness absolute where the company sat among the rocks without fire or bread or camaraderie any more than banded apes. They crouched in silence eating raw meat the Delawares had killed on the plain with arrows and they slept among the bones. A lobeshaped moon rose over the black shapes of the mountain dimming out the eastern stars and along the nearby ridge the white blooms of flowering yuccas moved in the wind and in the night bats came from some nether part of the world to stand on leather wings like dark satanic hummingbirds and feed at the mouths of those flowers. Farther along the ridge and slightly elevated on a ledge of sandstone squatted the judge, pale and naked. He raised is hand and the bats flared in confusion and then he lowered it and sat as before and soon they were feeding again.

This is an image of Walpurgis Night, the bats flying up like witches paying homage to their master, their judge the devil. McCarthy's narrative prose, always formal and latinate, is here heightened to a macabre and gothic intensity. Without this symbolic development the judge would appear merely a psychotic, brilliantly intellectual egomaniac, as here, in his disquisition on war:

It makes no difference what men think of war, said the judge. War endures. As well ask men what they think of stone. War was always here. Before man was, war waited for him. The ultimate trade awaiting its ultimate practitioner. That is the way it was and will be. That way and not some other way.

[…]

War is the ultimate game because war is at last a forcing of the unity of existence. War is god.

Through the symbolic development of the judge, the novel becomes a double parable: first, a particular parable of the 'winning of the west' under the guise of manifest destiny, whose basic concepts were the exceptional virtues of Americans and their institutions, the holiness of God's inspiration for America's actions, and America's mission to save the world by remaking it in the image of America. The second parable is the more general one of the ubiquity of violence and bloodshed in human history past and present.

Write a scene

Write a 250–300-word third-person introduction into a scene of someone very destructive, yet interesting.

Edit exercise

Write a 500-word description of an incident involving the character introduced in the exercise above. This should be described by another character who witnessed the incident.

The use of satire

Satire in fiction may be general or specific. An example of a general satire is Robert Coover's short story 'The Babysitter', in which male sexual fantasy is satirized by a sequence of increasingly improbable incidents, the storyline becoming positively deliquescent towards its climax. A famous example of specific satire is Sinclair Lewis's novel *Babbit*, which takes aim at the crassly sentimental, crudely materialistic life of the mid-level midwestern American businessman in all his big-cliché-mouthed glory.

Fictional satire has many formal means of presentation. Here are two different approaches, both satirizing college presidents.

SATIRE THROUGH NARRATIVE

The novel *Pictures from an Institution*, published in 1954, was written by the poet and critic Randall Jarrell. It satirizes the character of a progressive small college and its characters. Most of the satire is created through the narrative voice, that of an English faculty member. The 'Gertrude' referred to in the extract is his acquaintance, the visiting novelist Gertrude Johnson, known for her acid wit.

> *...President Robbins had what people called a rich full life. He had so many friends that, as Gertrude said, 'they fell over each other going out the door'.*
>
> [...]
>
> *Of course the President's friends didn't like him as well as many of our enemies like us, but they took pleasure in his misfortunes, were confidential with him when they had drunk so much of his liquor they couldn't see who he was, accepted favors willingly – they were normal Presidential friends, the mean or median or average friends of all very important people.*
>
> *Ordinary people think that very important people get along badly with one another – and this is true; but they*

often get along worse with you and me. They find it difficult not simply to get along with, but to care about getting along with, ordinary people, who do not seem to them fully human. They make exceptions, real or seeming, for school friends, people who flatter them enough, relatives, mistresses, children, and dogs: they try not to bite the hand that lets them stroke it... but all power irritates – it is hard for them to contain themselves within themselves, and not to roast the peasants on their slopes. But they eye one another with half-contemptuous, half-respectful dislike; after all, each of them is important, and importance, God knows, covers a multitude of sins.

Gertrude Johnson could feel no real respect for, no real interest in, anybody who wasn't a writer. For her there were two species: writers and people; and the writers were really people, and the people weren't. But unless we are very uncommon men, you and I split up the world in some analogous way; as Goethe has said, But who is so cultured as to refrain from cruelly stressing, at times, the qualities in which he excels? *And in this connection, no quality is so popular as that of having no particular qualities at all. The great – who may or may not be very important people – do not seem to most of us fully human.*

President Robbins, judge him as you please, was not human. He had not had time to be; besides, his own gift was for seeming human. He had taught sociology only a year, and during the last three months of that year he had already been selected to be Dean of Men at _____; two years later he was appointed Dean of the College of Arts and Sciences at _____; in six years he was President of Benton. They had *selected him. But how had they known whom to select? Would someone else have done as well? Why had they selected* just *him?*

If you ask this, you have never selected or been selected; you would know, then. Such questions are as ridiculous as asking how stigmata know who to select – as asking, 'Wouldn't somebody else have done as well as St. Francis?' A vocation, a *calling – these words apply quite as well in secular affairs as in religious. Luther knew. Have you yourself never known on of these* idiots savants *of success, of getting Ahead in the World? About other things they may know something or they may not, but about the World they have forgotten – in previous existences for which, perhaps, they are being punished? – far more than you or I will ever learn.*

President Robbins was, of course, one of these men. He 'did not have his PhD' – but had that bothered one administrator upon this earth? All had been as refreshingly unprejudiced about his lack of one as the President of Benton now was about anybody's possession of one. But at Benton all of them were like this; they looked up your degrees so they could tell you that, whatever the things were, they didn't mind. President Robbins had an MA from Oxford – he had been a Rhodes Scholar – and an LLD granted, in 1947, by Menuire. (It's a college in Florida.) To make the President dislike you for the rest of his life, say to him with a resigned anthropological smile: 'I've just been reading that in 1948 Menuire College gave the degree of Doctor of Humor to Milton Berle.'

The difference between the narrator's satire and Gertrude's is that hers is exclusive and his is inclusive. She quips about Robbins' large circle of friends that 'they fell over each other going out the door'. This is entirely directed at Robbins and his 'friends' who can't get away from the man fast enough. The narrator's first thrust: 'Of course the President's friends didn't like him as well as many of our enemies like *us*' – is just as vitriolic but draws us, the narrator and you and me the readers, into complicity with the narrator that he goes on to develop on the understanding that *we're* the ordinary folk against whom the extraordinary President stands out, stands shoulders above, is not of our ilk at all.

One source of Jarrell's wit is his variations, sometimes inversions, sometimes not, of well-known sayings. When he says that Robbins' friends nonetheless really acted like friends since they 'took pleasure in his misfortunes, were confidential with him when they had drunk so much of his liquor they couldn't see who he was', and so on, he's beginning with the old observation that 'we take pleasure in the *minor* misfortunes of our friends', omitting 'minor' and adding on his own list of meanness, ending up with calling these 'normal Presidential friends, the mean or median or average friends of all very important people'. Here, he's literally able to put in the word 'mean' by quickly qualifying it with the synonyms 'median' and 'average' so that we know he means the meaner meaning of 'mean'.

This leads him into a short diversion about how little we understand about very important people. It's a variation on the famous reply by Hemingway to Scott Fitzgerald's 'The rich are different from us' – 'Yes, they have more money.' As opposed to Hemingway's deflation of the 'specialness' of the rich, Jarrell, in his superficially playful way, makes the very important so special, so different, that they can't get along with anyone, really, but especially with us not very important people. He ends with two very funny parodies of stock sayings, turning 'All power corrupts' into 'all power irritates', and 'Don't bite the hand that feeds you', after listing possible exceptions to whom the very important dislike, ending with 'mistresses, children and dogs', into 'they try not to bite the hand that lets them stroke it'.

The entire diversion (itself reminiscent of *Tristram Shandy*) ends with 'The great – who may or may not be very important people – do not seem to most of *us* fully human.' This leads into the opening of his next paragraph: 'President Robbins, judge him as you please, was not human.' The brilliance here is the little, throwaway 'judge him as you please', as if this were a possibility under the stated condition of his being 'not human'. Then Jarrell offers Robbins the mock excuse 'He had not had time to be', and a second, bigger barb – 'besides, his own gift was for seeming human'. Wonderful stuff, this, making hypocrisy a 'gift'!

There is not a line of this narrative that isn't full of quietly sizzling wit. The more it excuses its target Robbins, the more it skewers him as the perfectly empty, smiling administrator, institutionalized, dehumanized.

SATIRE THROUGH DIALOGUE

A different formal approach to satire of a college president occurs near the start of Don DeLilo's early novel *End Zone,* published in 1972. Its first-person narrator is a US football-scholarship student at a small west Texas college called Logos. Because he's from New York state, he's been asked to the office of the college president to welcome the first black student ever to be enrolled, a great football player from New York City. Rather than through narrative, the satire here is, with one notable descriptive exception, achieved through the character of the president herself, in dialogue.

I was in the president's office the day he arrived. The president was Mrs Tom Wade, the founder's widow. Everybody called her Mrs Tom. She was the only woman I had ever seen who might accurately be described as Lincolnesque. Beyond appearance I had no idea of her reality: she was tall, black-browed, stark as a railroad spike.

[...]

Mrs Tom and I sat waiting.

'My husband loved this place,' she said. 'He built it out of nothing. He had an idea and he followed it through to the end. He believed in reason. He was a man of reason. He cherished the very word. Unfortunately he was mute.'

'I didn't know that.'

'All he could do was grunt. He made disgusting sounds. Spit used to collect at both corners of his mouth. It wasn't a real pretty sight.'

Taft [the black student] walked in flanked by our head coach, Emmet Creed, and backfield coach, Oscar Veech.

[...]

Mrs Tom made her speech.

'Young man, I have always admired the endurance of your people. You've had a tough row to hoe. Frankly I was against this from the start. When they told me their plan, I said it was bushwah. Complete bushwah. But Emmet Creed is a mighty persuasive man. This won't be easy for any of us. But what's reason for if not to get us through the hard times? There now. I've had my say. Now you go on ahead with Coach Creed and when you're all thoo talking football you be sure to come on back here and see Mrs Berry Trout next door. She'll get you all settled on courses and accommodations and things. History will be our ultimate judge.'

Only the president's physical description is narrative satire. The president, wife of the first president and founder, Tom Wade, doesn't even get her own *married* name but is called simply Mrs Tom. The narrator finds this strangely male-named lady the only woman he's seen who can be described as 'Lincolnesque', literally describing these characteristics as 'tall, black-browed, stark as a railroad spike'. He makes a point of emphasizing his meaning of 'Lincolnesque' as solely her 'appearance'. What he's left out, of course, is the beard – Lincoln's, not Mrs Tom's. Mrs Tom is, after all, a woman who's Lincolnesque, but you can't help seeing that beard in this description. He doesn't have to comment on Mrs Tom suggesting Mr Tom, which suggests Uncle Tom.

The great hilarious deadpan bulk of the satire comes from the mouth of Mrs Tom herself. First, there's the conventional dignity of her opening remarks: how her husband built the college from nothing; how he had an idea and followed it to its end; how he believed in reason (Logos). She continues with deeper feeling: how he was a man of reason, how he 'cherished the very word'. Then comes the slight surprise of 'Unfortunately, he was mute.'

This catches you off guard; you can only think what the narrator voices – 'I didn't know that.'

Her next sequence is jaw-droppingly wild: 'All he could do was grunt. He made disgusting sounds. Spit used to collect at both corners of his mouth. It wasn't a real pretty sight.' You can almost hear the second-long beat of Pinteresque silence between 'his mouth' and 'It wasn't a real pretty sight.' Note, too, the first presence of colloquial speech at that bitter end – not 'real' pretty. She's let her guard down.

Next comes her speech of welcome to the college's first black student, Taft Robinson, the football star. She first compliments the 'endurance of your people'. Yes, they have had to endure the treatment of her people. As if her implied reference to her admiration of how his people had put up with slavery and what followed is not clear enough, she adds the outrageously literal level of the metaphorical cliché, 'You've a tough row to hoe.' She follows this with another punishing statement that she's been against his enrolling at this all-white school, said when first told that 'it was bushwah. Complete bushwah.' President Mrs Tom uses 'bushwah' as a euphemism for 'bullshit'. Then she promises him a hard time, as hard for him to be here as it will be for her to know that he's here. And after she's had 'her say', her stern and forthright say, her tone seems to change with 'you be sure to come on back here', the colloquial returning to her speech in 'come on back', the traditional warm goodbye of the south with its promise of further personal hospitality. Except it isn't, she's telling him to return 'next door' to the wonderfully named administrator Mrs Berry Trout, who you may suspect will be another cold fish.

Out of her own Lincolnesque mouth (the beard? the beard?), she goes down fighting: 'History will be our ultimate judge', she says to the strangely named Taft Robinson, half Jackie Robinson, the first black baseball player in the major leagues. He is half William Howard Taft or Robert Taft, Republican president and senator respectively of a different sort of Republican than Lincoln who freed the slaves.

This is pretty much all we see of Mrs Tom in the novel. But she is a memorable character and memorable satire of the straight-faced, fantastic variety.

Write character satire

Write two pieces of character satire, about 350 words each. In one, do this through first- or third-person narration. In the other piece, write it so that the character herself/himself unknowingly creates the satire. Be clear, as you write, about what or whom you are satirizing.

Workshop

Using the first writing exercise in this chapter, apply your analysis of symbolic potential for one of your characters that you haven't treated in any symbolic way. Now write a scene for this character, which includes one or more symbolic elements in the character's development. Remember, the symbol should first work at the literal level. When you've finished a first draft, consider it in the light of your original analysis as a means of revision and editing in a second draft.

Focus points

- The use of symbolism is an important way of revealing character.
- Rounded character development is difficult in allegory, where one-to-one equivalence between story elements and symbolic meanings typically demands a flattening of character. Parable offers more scope for character development since it can represent an overall moral, social or historical meaning which the writer usually maintains as a truth.

- A symbolic character can represent the writer's message and turn the story into a parable.
- Satire in fiction targets human weakness through the use of humour or wit.
- Satire may be general or specific and be presented through narrative or dialogue.

Next step

The book's final chapter asks you to look at two pieces of great character development. One is achieved by 'voice', and one is achieved by climactic action that constitutes a 'turning moment' in the character's life.

8

Character: voice and turning point

'Voice' is obviously narration, but its focus is literally the sound to your reading ear that communicates character, the 'living' person who tells you the story, their own or others'. A narrator can use metaphor, cliché, interjections and other devices to tell you, the reader, things that they themselves might not be aware of.

A turning point is where the elements of character interaction and development in the story lead to a point of maximum tension or conflict, where a character is forced to change his or her behaviour and then go in a new direction. The turning point leads to a new self-knowledge in the protagonist. The best turning moments involve a character who's been written so that you understand both the potential for such change *and* the aspects of character that could keep him from changing, or even make him change for the worse.

Voice and character

This story, an example of perfect voice, is **'Where I'm Calling From'**, by Raymond Carver (1988). The excerpts below are sequential and numbered for reference. The first excerpt is the opening of the story. It's longer than others to accustom you to the narrator's voice.

EXCERPT 1

J.P. and I are on the front porch of Frank Martin's drying-out facility. Like the rest of us at Frank Martin's, J.P. is first and foremost a drunk. But he's also a chimney sweep. It's his first time here, and he's scared. I've been here once before. What's to say? I'm back. J.P.'s real name is Joe Penny, but he says I should call him J.P. He's about thirty years old. Younger than I am. Not much younger, but a little. He's telling me how he decided to go into his line of work, and he wants to use his hands when he talks. But his hands tremble. I mean, they won't keep still. 'This has never happened to me before,' he says. He means the trembling. I tell him I sympathize. I tell him the shakes will idle down. And they will. But it takes time.

We've only been in here a couple of days. We're not out of the woods yet. J.P. has these shakes, and every so often a nerve – maybe it isn't a nerve, but it's something – begins to jerk in my shoulder. Sometimes it's at the side of my neck. When this happens, my mouth dries up. It's an effort just to swallow then. I know something's about to happen and I want to head it off. I want to hide from it, that's what I want to do. Just close my eyes and let it pass by, let it take the next man. J.P. can wait a minute.

I saw a seizure yesterday morning. A guy called Tiny. A big fat guy, an electrician from Santa Rosa. They said he'd been in here for nearly two weeks and that he was over the hump. He was going home in a day or two and would spend New Year's Eve with his wife in front of the TV. On New Year's Eve, Tiny planned to drink hot chocolate and eat cookies. Yesterday morning he seemed just fine when he came down for breakfast. He was letting out with quacking noises, showing some guy how he called ducks right down onto his head. 'Blam, Blam,' said Tiny, picking off a couple.

*Tiny's hair was damp and was slicked back along the sides
of his head. He'd just come out of the shower. He'd also
nicked himself on the chin with his razor. But so what? Just
about everybody at Frank Martin's has nicks on his face. It's
something that happens. Tiny edged in at the head of the
table and began telling about something that had happened
on one of his drinking bouts. People at the table laughed and
shook their heads as they shoveled up their eggs. Tiny would
say something, grin, then look around the table for a sign of
recognition. We'd all done things just as bad and crazy, so,
sure, that's why we laughed. Tiny had some scrambled eggs on
his plate, and some biscuits and honey. I was at the table, but
I wasn't hungry. I had some coffee in front of me. Suddenly,
Tiny wasn't there anymore. He'd gone over in his chair with
a big clatter. He was on his back on the floor with his eyes
closed, his heels drumming the linoleum. People hollered
for Frank Martin. But he was right there. A couple of guys
got down on the floor beside Tiny. One of the guys put his
fingers inside Tiny's mouth and tried to hold his tongue. Frank
Martin yelled, 'Everybody stand back!' Then I noticed that
the bunch of us were leaning over Tiny, just looking at him,
not able to take our eyes off him. 'Give him air!' Frank Martin
said. Then he ran into the office and called the ambulance.*

*Tiny is on board again today. Talk about bouncing back.
This morning Frank Martin drove the station wagon to the
hospital to get him. Tiny got back too late for his eggs, but
he took some coffee into the dining room and sat down at
the table anyway. Somebody in the kitchen made toast for
him, but Tiny didn't eat it. He just sat with his coffee and
looked into his cup. Every now and then he moved his cup
back and forth in front of him.*

*I'd like to ask him if he had any signal just before it
happened. I'd like to know if he felt his ticker skip a beat,
or else begin to race. Did his eyelid twitch? But I'm not
about to say anything. He doesn't look like he's hot to talk
about it, anyway. But what happened to Tiny is something
I won't ever forget. Old Tiny flat on the floor, kicking his
heels. So every time this little flitter starts up anywhere,
I draw some breath and wait to find myself on my back,
looking up, somebody's fingers in my mouth.*

156

The narrator uses clichés like 'first and foremost' and 'We're not out of the woods yet'. You can find others. What is Carver doing? How are these clichés effective? Is it only to establish the ordinariness of the narrator, the suggestion of background, education, etc? I hear 'first and foremost' as powerful and original in this context: 'Like the rest of us at Frank Martin's, J.P. is first and foremost a drunk.' Why?

The narrator says of J.P., 'It's his first time here, and he's scared.' In these five paragraphs he never uses 'scared' or its synonyms again, yet it's the underlying, driving emotion of all of this extract. Can you see and hear that? What's the closest the narrator comes to saying this about himself?

Use clichés and interjections to develop character

Write a 750-word opening to a piece of fiction with first-person narration in which the narrator is *telling*, rather than *writing*, a story. Have the narrator use clichés and self-conscious interjections so that your reader begins to get a feel for what's important to the narrator without it being explicitly stated.

Do you think Frank Martin would mind being referred to as just 'Frank'? Why does the narrator always refer to him as 'Frank Martin' rather than 'Frank'?

There are a number of odd breaks in the narrative. In order of appearance they are: 'What's to say?' and 'But so what?' and 'sure' in the sentence 'We'd all done things just as bad and crazy, so, sure, that's why we laughed.' What are these doing? That is, how is Carver developing his character with these apparently self-conscious interjections?

In the story's next section, the narrator listens to J.P. talk and urges him on. He tells us what J.P. is saying. First, J.P. speaks of an accident he had when he was 12 years old. Walking along over a field he suddenly fell into a dry well and waited for a long time at the bottom until he was lucky enough for his father to come along and haul him out with a rope. He had been all alone down there for a long while, and he could see only, way up, 'a circle of blue sky' or a passing cloud. He wet himself while waiting. Birds flew overhead, setting insects to moving and rustle in the earth above him. When J.P. ends this story, the narrator says, 'keep talking, J.P. Then what?'

Next, J.P. tells him a longer story, starting when he's just out of high school at 18 or so and goes over to a friend's house to hang around. The parents aren't in. The two of them drink beer, talk and listen to records. Then a young woman chimney sweep wearing a top hat arrives: the friend's parents have arranged this and have left a cheque to give her when she's through. J.P. is immediately struck with her looks. As she cleans, the boys watch her, grinning and winking at each other. When she's finished the friend gives her the cheque, at which she asks him whether he wants a kiss. 'It's supposed to bring good luck,' she explains. The friend is embarrassed and clowns about; then he kisses her cheek. But J.P. follows her to the door and asks for a kiss, too. The young woman, Roxy, looks him over and says, 'Why not? I've got some extra kisses.' Then the narrator says:

EXCERPT 2

And she kissed him a good one right on his lips and then turned to go.

Like that, quick as a wink, J.P. followed her on to the porch. He held the porch screen door for her. He went down the steps with her and out to the drive, where she'd parked her panel truck. It was something that was out of his hands. Nothing else in the world counted for anything. He knew that he's met somebody who could set his legs atremble. He could feel her kiss still burning on his lips, etc. J.P. couldn't begin to sort anything out. He was filled with sensations that were carrying him every which way.

He opened the rear door of the panel truck for her. He helped her store her things inside. 'Thanks,' she told him. Then he blurted it out – that he'd like to see her again. Would she go to a movie with him sometime? He realized, too, what he wanted to do with his life. He wanted to do what she did. He wanted to be a chimney sweep. But he didn't tell her that then.

J.P. says she put her hands on her hips and looked him over. Then she found a business card in the front seat of her truck. She gave it to him. She said, 'Call this number after ten tonight. We can talk. I have to go now.' She put the top hat on and then took it off. She looked at J.P. once more. She must have liked what she saw, because this time she grinned. He told her there was a smudge near her mouth. Then she got into her truck, tooted her horn, and drove away.

'Then what?' I say. 'Don't stop now, J.P.'

I was interested. But I would have listened if he'd been going on about how one day he'd decided to start pitching horseshoes.

Carver doesn't have the narrator explain this last sentence: his character is neither a writer nor a professional storyteller. So it's the reader who works out that the narrator is desperate to keep listening to keep his mind off what he wants to think about – his enormous need to have a drink. At this point, J.P. pauses and continues, and the narrator goes on to relate how J.P. starts going out with Roxy, slowly talks her into letting him go along with her to her jobs, and the courtship develops as they sweep chimneys together. Soon they marry, and Roxy's father makes him a full partner in the business. In a year, Roxy has a baby and stops being a sweep. Soon there's another child. J.P. buys a house, adores his wife and kids and is happy with his life.

Then – and he can't explain why – he starts drinking more and more beer, then gin and tonic while he watches TV, then more and more gin and tonic through the day and night, stopping off at a bar to drink before dinner. Then he starts missing dinners or turns up late but isn't hungry, having filled up on bar snacks. He then starts getting angry, throws his lunch pail across the room, and when Roxy yells at him he storms out and goes to the bar to drink again. He begins drinking in the morning, takes a thermos of vodka with him in his lunch pail. He and Roxy fight. She hits him in the face and breaks his nose. Now they fight in front of the kids. Roxy finds a boyfriend, and J.P., finding out, gets the wedding ring off her finger and cuts it to bits with his cutter. The next morning he's arrested on a drunk driving charge. He loses his licence and can't drive to work any more. 'Just as well,' he says. He's already fallen off a roof and broken his thumb. He says it was just a matter of time until he broke his neck.

During this talk, J.P. stops once. The narrator says, 'He just clams up. What's going on? I'm listening. It's helping me relax, for one thing. It's taking me away from my own situation. After a minute, I say, "What the hell? Go on, J.P."' Here, the narrator makes explicit what he meant when, in excerpt 2, he said, 'I would have listened if he'd been going on about how one day he'd decided to start pitching horseshoes.' The narrator's agenda is to keep being distracted so that he doesn't think of himself, of those twitches that could signal a seizure, of the drunken mess he's made of his own life.

But what else connects J.P.'s story to the narrator's? You assume that J.P. isn't making this up. So why does Carver, the writer, decide to have J.P. fall down a dry well when he was 12? Just be walking along a field and suddenly find himself at the bottom of a well he can't climb out of. And what about those details – being able to see a circle of blue sky and the occasional cloud and some birds, and the sound of insects moving around just over his head? The incident is like a metaphor of both J.P. and the narrator's lives, though they wouldn't understand it as 'metaphor'. It's like one day they wake up drunks and the solid earth has given way beneath their feet and they can't get out of the hole they're in, not on their own, yet they can see the real world above them.

The next excerpt returns to the narrator telling of his arrival at Frank Martin's.

EXCERPT 3

As I said, this is my second time at Frank Martin's. When I was trying to sign a check to pay in advance for a week's stay, Frank Martin said, 'The holidays are always bad. Maybe you should think of sticking around a little longer this time? Think in terms of a couple of weeks. Can you do a couple of weeks? Think about it, anyway. You don't have to decide anything now,' he said. He held his thumb on the check and I signed my name. Then I walked my girlfriend to the front door and said goodbye. 'Goodbye,' she said, and she lurched into the doorjamb and then on to the porch. It's late afternoon. It's raining. I go from the door to the window. I move the curtain and watch her drive away. She's in my car. She's drunk. But I'm drunk, too, and there's nothing I can do. I make it to a big chair that's close to the radiator, and I sit down. Some guys look up from their TV. Then they shift back to what they were watching. I just sit there. Now and then I look up at something that's happening on the screen.

Later that afternoon the front door banged open and J.P. was brought in between these two big guys – his father-in-law and brother-in-law, I find out afterward. [They sign J.P. in, pay a check, and help him up to bed.]

*Pretty soon the old guy and the other guy came downstairs
and headed for the front door. They couldn't seem to get
out of this place fast enough. It was like they couldn't wait
to wash their hands of all this. I didn't blame them. Hell,
no. I don't know how I'd act if I was in their shoes.*

Returning to the present, the narrator relates how he and J.P. are
sitting out on the porch when Frank Martin comes out and points
across the valley and tells them that Jack London's big house used
to be behind the green hill over there. He says, 'But alcohol killed
him. Let that be a lesson to you. He was a better man than any of
us. But he couldn't handle the stuff, either.' He then recommends
London's *The Call of the Wild*, if they want to read something
while they're here.

EXCERPT 4

*'I feel like a bug when he's around,' J.P. says. 'He makes
me feel like a bug.' J.P. shakes his head. Then he says, 'Jack
London. What a name! I wish I had me a name like that.
Instead of the name I got.'*

This is the most revealing statement J.P. makes: he, like the narrator,
doesn't really believe in himself; he believes in some other, some
outside force, some luck, some magic, like if he only had a name like
Jack London he'd be okay, cured, back out of the pit on solid ground.

The narrator then tells how it was his wife who brought him up here
the first time. She talked with Frank Martin 'for an hour or two'
before she left. He continues:

EXCERPT 5

*This time around, it was my girlfriend who drove me here.
She was driving my car. She drove us through a rainstorm.
We drank champagne all the way. We were both drunk
when she pulled up in the drive. She intended to drop me
off, turn around, and drive home again. She had things to
do. One thing she had to do was to go to work the next
day. She was a secretary. She had an okay job with this
electronic-parts firm. She also had this mouthy teenaged
son. I wanted her to get a room in town, spend the night,
and then drive home. I don't know if she got the room or
not. I haven't heard from her since she led me up the front*

steps the other day and walked me into Frank Martin's office and said, 'Guess who's here.'

But I wasn't mad at her. In the first place, she didn't have any idea what she was letting herself in for when she said I could stay with her after my wife asked me to leave. I felt sorry for her. The reason I felt sorry for her was that on the day before Christmas her Pap smear came back, and the news was not cheery. She'd have to go back to the doctor, and real soon. That kind of news was reason enough for both of us to start drinking. So what we did was get ourselves good and drunk. And on Christmas Day we were still drunk. We had to go out to a restaurant to eat, because we didn't feel like cooking. The two of us and her mouthy teenaged son opened some presents, and then we went to this steakhouse near her apartment. I wasn't hungry. I had some soup and a hot roll. I drank a bottle of wine with the soup. She drank some wine, too. Then we started in on Bloody Marys. For the next couple of days, I didn't eat anything except salted nuts. But I drank a lot of bourbon. Then I said to her, 'Sugar, I think I'd better pack up. I better go back to Frank Martin's.'

She tried to explain to her son that she was going to be gone for a while and he'd have to get his own food. But right as we were gong out the door, this mouthy kid screamed at us. He screamed, 'The hell with you! I hope you never come back. I hope you kill yourselves!' Imagine this kid!

And on New Year's morning the narrator tries to call his wife, but there's no answer. He says how the last time they'd spoken they screamed at each other and she hung up on him. He then brings in another character.

EXCERPT 6

One of the guys here is a guy who travels. He goes to Europe and places. That's what he says, anyway. Business, he says. He also says he has his drinking under control and he doesn't have any idea why he's here at Frank Martin's. But he doesn't remember getting here. He laughs about it, about his not remembering. 'Anyone can have a blackout,' he says. 'That doesn't prove a thing.' He's not a drunk – he tells us this and we listen. 'That's a serious charge to make,' he says. 'That kind of talk can ruin a good man's prospects.' He says that if he'd only stick to whiskey and water, no ice, he'd never have these blackouts. It's the ice they put into your drink that does it. 'Who do you know in Egypt?' he asks me. 'I can use a few names over there.'

This 'Who do you know in Egypt' is funny and pathetic at the same time. The drunk has no idea who he's speaking to, and the narrator is terrified of commenting on what the reader would call the delusional depths of the alcoholic businessman, as the narrator struggles to keep from falling into them.

J.P. tells the narrator that his wife, Roxy, is coming to visit him the next day, New Year's Day. Then the narrator goes to the phone and tries to call his wife collect, but again there's no answer. Then he thinks of calling his girlfriend but realizes he doesn't want to talk to her. He says, 'I hope she's okay. But if she has something wrong with her, I don't want to know about it.'

On New Year's Day morning, J.P. and the narrator sit out on the porch waiting for Roxy to arrive. J.P. tells him she asked if she should bring the kids but he said no. He says, 'Can you imagine? My God, I don't want my kids up here.' They smoke and 'look across the valley to where Jack London used to live', and then the car drives up.

EXCERPT 7

I see this woman stop the car and set the brake. I see J.P. open the door. I watch her get out, and I see them hug each other. I look away. Then I look back. J.P. takes her by the arm and they come up the stairs. This woman broke a man's nose once. She has had two kids and much trouble, but she loves this man who has her by the arm. I get up from the chair.

The narrator finds her good looking. He tells her that J.P. has told him how they met. There's some small talk, some friendly joking from Roxy about what J.P. has and hasn't told him. Then this:

EXCERPT 8

Then they start to go inside. I know it's a dumb thing to do, but I do it anyway. 'Roxy,' I say. And they stop in the doorway and look at me. 'I need some luck,' I say. 'No kidding. I could do with a kiss myself.'

J.P. looks down. He's still holding the knob, even though the door is open. He turns the knob back and forth. But I keep looking at her. Roxy grins. 'I'm not a sweep anymore,' she says. 'Not for years. Didn't Joe tell you that? But, sure, I'll kiss you, sure.'

She moves over. She takes me by the shoulders – I'm a big man – and she plants this kiss on my lips. 'How's that?' she says.

'That's fine,' I say.

'Nothing to it,' she says. She's still holding me by the shoulders. She's looking me right in the eyes. 'Good luck,' she says, and then lets go of me.

'See you later, pal,' J.P. says. He opens the door all the way, and they go in.

Here it is, the narrator's desperate need for 'luck', for some force outside himself to pull him out of his mess, as, at the heart of things, he understands that he alone can't do it.

The narrator then sits and thinks of chimney sweeps, and that makes him think of a house his wife and he once lived in, though it had no chimney, and that makes him think of one morning when they lay in bed while an old man, their landlord, continued to paint on a ladder outside the bedroom window while they continued to make love.

Finally, he breaks off from this reverie and thinks he'll call his wife later this New Year's Day. And maybe, later, his girlfriend, hoping 'her mouthy kid' won't pick up the phone. He remembers he once read a Jack London story in high school, 'To Build a Fire', about a man in the Yukon who's fallen through ice and wet his socks and shoes. He's on his own, except for his dog, and unless he can get a fire going to dry his clothes, he'll freeze to death. It's getting colder and colder in the story, the narrator remembers, and night is coming on. Then he thinks he'll call his wife; he'll have to tell her where he's calling from. He won't lose his temper. Then he thinks maybe he'll call his girlfriend first. The story ends in a frenzy of indecision.

What's the advantage, in excerpt 3 above, to character development of Carver writing, 'I was trying to write a check,' and, later in the paragraph, 'He held his thumb on the check and I signed my name', rather than having the narrator describe his shakes directly?

Also in excerpt 3, referring to J.P.'s in-laws bringing him into Frank Martin's, the narrator says, 'It was like they couldn't wait to wash their hands of all this. I didn't blame them. Hell, no.' Do the last two statements seem genuine or a rationalization, that is, a way of kidding himself that he isn't a drunk?

Excerpt 4 has Frank Martin suggesting the narrator and J.P. read Jack London's *The Call of the Wild,* a novel in which the heroic half-dog, half-wolf overcomes terrific odds to survive and finally run free. At the story's end, the narrator recalls a Jack London story he read in high school, in which the freezing man up in the Yukon cannot light a fire to dry his clothes and so will die, though he doesn't speak literally of the story's end. So if you know the London novel you'll immediately feel the dark, lost mood of the narrator at the story's end. Yet it's pretty clear, since he never refers to the novel again after saying that Frank Martin recommended it, that the narrator doesn't know the novel and, of course, can't see the shift between Frank Martin's positive attitude and his own growing depression. What does Carver want to do here?

If you go back to my summary statement just before excerpt 5 and then read excerpt 5, what differences do you find that reveal something about the narrator's character in relation to how his wife and his girlfriend act with him on delivering him to the drying-out facility?

Why is the narrator never named?

- The narrator is not a particularly nice man. It's clear that he had a girlfriend to live with when his wife kicked him out.
- He's not a sensitive man. His girlfriend's son has ample provocation to be 'mouthy': his drunk mother has shacked up with a drunk guy who makes her drunker. She can't even cook something for Christmas. Then this guy takes her away on Christmas day, just like that. Of course the boy is hurt and angry. The narrator has no feeling for what the boy is going through.
- Moreover, the narrator is selfish even with his 'pal' J.P. He listens to J.P.'s story primarily to keep his mind off his own story – of troubles.

So why are readers so sympathetic to this narrator? (They are.) Is it his attitude towards 'the mouthy teenaged kid' that makes you feel that the narrator and his wife have no children?

Edit exercise

Take the writing exercise you did earlier in this chapter and, keeping the same story idea, rewrite the character of your first-person narrator by presenting him/her as more self-assured and self-concealing. Its clichés should be different, more 'educated', and any interjections or interruptions to the narrative flow should be, at least superficially, less self-conscious than your original narrator's.

Turning points and character

The term 'turning point' or 'turning moment' is used here rather than 'climax' to focus on character. A reason for using it is that 'climax' doesn't necessarily mean that the characters involved must change because of it. My interest is to show you elements of character interaction and development that lead to a turning-point moment and that then go from this moment in a new direction – yet one compatible with character development prior to this.

In Richard Ford's novel *Independence Day* (1995), its narrator and central character, Frank Bascombe, ex-sportswriter, ex-short-storywriter, now realtor, divorced and whose two children live with their mother, takes his problematic 15-year-old son Paul on a boy's own sporting hall-of-fame car trip over the 48 hours of the 4 July Independence Day weekend. Having spent its Friday night with his lady friend Sally, Frank is making a real though somewhat belated effort to bond with his adolescent, hormone-tormented son. He is doing this by, among other things, casually assigning Paul preparatory reading in the form of Emerson's *Self-Reliance* and a 'classic' sociopolitical interpretation of the Declaration of Independence. He does this so that he and Paul can discuss in depth the deeper meanings of the weekend's celebrations, hoping that this might help Paul through his current predicaments.

Paul has been arrested for shoplifting giant-sized condoms and assaulting the woman security guard who attempted to detain him. He's due in court on 5 July, the Tuesday after the weekend. Paul is also troubled by memories of the long-ago death of the family basset hound and, beneath that, of the death of his brother Ralph from a rare childhood disease. And, of course, Paul deeply resents his parents' breakup and his mother's smooth new husband Charley O'Dell. Paul makes strange squeaking sounds sometimes; he barks sometimes; sometimes in a high piping voice he cries 'Save me, save me!'

Frank, despite his unrealistic over-planning, is an attractive character: articulate, literate, witty and funny. But he hasn't spent enough time with his son during these suddenly testosterone-crowded years. The divorce had Frank nursing his own wounded ego by going off to live in France, joining a real-men's-only woodsports fishing club and hooking up with various women – before finding Sally – for one-night stands. But with no day-after-day living with his needy son, there are now strong distress signals. Ex-wife Ann has sent Paul to a camp for troubled teens at which he's been diagnosed, as Frank puts it: 'even though he [Paul] acts and talks like a shrewd sophomore in the honors program at Beloit, full of sly jokes and double entendres (he has also recently shot up to 5'8", with a new layer of quaky pudge all over), his feelings still get hurt in the manner of a child who knows much less about the world than a Girl Scout.'

Besides the 'casual' seminar on Emerson and the Founding Document, here's what Frank plans for the buddies weekend:

> *...bright and early tomorrow I am picking him up all the way in Connecticut and staging for both of our benefits a split-the-breeze father-and-son driving campaign in which we will visit as many sports halls of fame as humanly possible in one forty-eight hour period (this being only two), winding up in storied Cooperstown, where we'll stay in the venerable Deerslayer Inn, fish on scenic Lake Otsego, shoot off safe and ethical fireworks, eat like castaways, and somehow along the way I'll work (I hope) the miracle only a father can work. Which is to say: if your son begins suddenly to fall at a headlong rate, you must through the agency of love and greater age throw him a line and haul him back. (All of this somehow before delivering him to his mother in NYC and getting myself back here to Haddam, where I myself, for reasons of familiarity, am best off on the 4th of July.)*

As if this weren't already an over-ambitious plan, Frank has more ideas for his son:

> *Naturally enough, I can explain almost nothing to him. Fatherhood by itself doesn't provide wisdom worth imparting. Though in preparation for our trip, I've sent him copies of* Self-Reliance *and the Declaration, and suggested*

he take a browse. These are not your ordinary fatherly offerings, I admit; yet I believe his instincts are sound and he will help himself if he can, and that independence is, in fact, what he lacks – independence from whatever holds him captive: memory, history, bad events he struggles with, can't control, but feels he should.

Even here, early in the novel, you feel that such overload should trigger a fuse to go off in Frank's way too illogically logical mind. He must, you feel, somewhere know that he can't cram years of daily absence into one short weekend. Telling, of course, is his belief in 'the miracle only a father can work' – that superstition. There's an early phone conversation between Frank and Paul, during which Paul calls his mother a bitch. Despite Frank's patiently explaining that she is not and that her life is, believe it or not, harder than his in that she has to deal with Paul, despite Frank's playing along with Paul's obsessive delight in puns by responding to him with further puns – despite, which really means *because of* this – you feel the tension between father and son. There's a desperate bonhomie that evokes literally and movingly the word 'divorce'. Frank is not only divorced from Ann but from Paul and his sister Clarissa.

Frank takes his time, not getting to the actual picking up of Paul until more than a quarter of the way through the novel, but you don't mind. Frank tells good stories about and against himself and his likes and loves and fears and failures. One incident bothers him for years and gives some insight to the novel's shaping of his character. Frank and Ann were leaving a professional basketball game in New York when a man appeared in the crowd waving a gun and threatening to shoot everyone. Frank instinctively made for the adjacent men's room, pulling Ann in behind him. Though the madman is quickly subdued by police without hurting anyone, Ann broods about what's happened. She points out that what he did was get behind her, leaving her, not himself, in the man's line of fire.

Frank tries to explain that he had to act with speed, and moving her 'behind him' would have taken time, and been awkward and ... He's bitter about how what he considered his quick-thinking heroism was interpreted by Ann as cowardice. He says, 'who wouldn't be bothered? ... My belief had always been with the ancient Greeks, that the most important events in life are physical events ... it appeared I'd pushed my dearest loved on in front of myself as cravenly as a slinking cur (appearances are just as bad when cowardice is at issue.)' This belief that action, not words, is most revealing of character is played out time and time again in the novel, to the extent that when staying in the Deerslayer Inn and, at loose ends, going to its rather musty library, Frank finds his one published book of short stories there and is first pleased to see it again, but when he finds a lipsticked-in argument between a couple behind the cover, he becomes furious and throws his book across the room. Moments like this reveal what he never admits, not even in his own thoughts, that he still feels bitter and maybe a pathetic failure for not trying harder with his first choice of career. This belief/trait will appear as a powerful force in the novel's turning moment.

As Frank comes closer to his wife's house, you read more potential trouble building up into this overcrowded weekend. He finds, on the phone, that Paul, the previous day, threw and hit his stepfather in the face with an oarlock, and told his mother, in front of the man, that she needed to get rid of 'asshole Charlie', then ran off and without a driving licence took his mother's car and almost immediately sideswiped an old oak tree on a neighbour's property, popping the airbag and cutting his ear. Paul's still abed when Frank arrives, so he first has a sweet talk with his daughter Clarissa and then a terrible argument with his ex, Ann. He tells Ann about his tight two-day schedule, starting at the Basketball Hall of Fame and ending that night in upstate New York at the Baseball Hall of Fame. Ann (not yet livid) points out that Paul is 'not really a big baseball fan, is he?' Frank, who will let nothing disturb his meticulous plans, replies, 'He knows more than you think he knows. Plus, going's the *ur*-father-son experience.' What's primary here, and throughout the weekend, is that Frank's own wishes are made more and more to dominate Paul's much more casual approach to time with his dad.

First, they drive up to Springfield, Massachusetts. Inside the Hall of Fame they pass a basket-shooting machine: a conveyor belt passes baskets at various distances, and basketballs come up into a trough by the belt. Frank decides they'll have a go, so Paul urges his father to go first, which he does. It looks simple enough to Frank until he begins. He ends up not being able to take many shots and not making one basket. Then Paul plays. He doesn't even bother taking a shot or even picking up a basketball. When his turn is finished, he tells Frank, without irony, that he's enjoyed it. Frank isn't expecting a basketball star, but this leaves him even more puzzled about his son.

Then, on the drive to upstate New York towards the Baseball Hall of Fame, Frank is delighted by the scenery, by how the geology shifts and presents one fine vista after another. But when he checks over at Paul, the boy is either sleeping or listening to something on his headphones or … or really being very difficult for Frank to reach.

But, at last, Paul starts flipping the pages of Emerson's *Self-Reliance*, and Frank sets to work. Paul asks Frank, '"What's this supposed to be about?" He stares down at the page he happens to have opened. "Is it a novel?"' Then he starts reading from it aloud 'in a psuedo-reverent Charlton Heston voice', interspersing 'blah, blahs', 'glub, glubs', and 'quack, quacks'. Frank tells him just to read it. 'There's not going to be a test.'

> *'Test. Tests make me really mad,' Paul says, and suddenly with his dirty fingers rips out the page he's read from.*
>
> *'Don't do that!' I make a grab for it, crunching the green cover so that I dent its shiny paper. 'You have to be a complete nitwit asshole to do that!' I stuff the book between my legs, though Paul still has the torn page and is folding it carefully into quarters. This qualifies as oppositional.*
>
> *'I'll keep it instead of remembering it.' He maintains his poise, while mine's all lost. He sticks the folded page into his shorts pocket and looks out his window the other way. I am glaring at him. 'I just took a page from your book.' He says this in his Heston voice. 'Do you by the way see yourself as a complete failure?'*

After calming down somewhat, Frank admits that his marriage and Paul's upbringing 'haven't been major accomplishments in my current term. Everything else is absolutely great, though', after which he notes, 'I am gaunt with how little I want to be in the car alone with my son, only barely arrived upon the storied streets of our destination.' Then Paul begins talking about the beloved family basset hound that died years back, and the mood apparently changes. When Paul says he just can't stop thinking about this, that it seemed to ruin everything 'that was fixed back then', Frank suggests he write down some of his thoughts about it.

> *'You mean a journal?' He eyes me dubiously.*
>
> *'Right. Like that.'*
>
> *'We did that at camp. Then we used our journals to wipe our asses and threw them in bonfires. That was the best use for them.'*

Notice that Ford makes Paul really obnoxious, from time to time, and that this makes you feel some sympathy for Frank's reactive behaviour. The point to understand as a writer is that this makes the reader somewhat complicit in the central character's *bad* behaviour.

Key idea

The job of the writer is to show and tell the truth, not to make the character nicer than he is or should be.

Write an incident

Write a 750-word piece based on a character from your fiction portfolio in which she or he narrates an incident with a family member or close friend who's behaving badly but where the narrator's reaction is another sort of bad or selfish or inappropriate behaviour *in keeping with her or his character*.

Arriving at the hotel, Frank immediately falls asleep. When he wakes, he's missed dinner and finds that Paul is gone. There is, in this natural-enough occurrence, something that typifies Frank: the difference between his elaborate, well-meaning plans and his irresponsibility in not carrying them through. In this case, he's lost the evening he's planned to spend with Paul. Nevertheless, the next morning they set out on foot for the Baseball Hall of Fame. When they get there, they find there's some sort of picket demonstration at its entrance. To Paul's suggestion that they simply skirt the group and go inside, Frank replies that the picket will probably end soon, so the two of them should just walk around for a short while and come back. Here, Frank, a 'New Deal' Democrat, doesn't explain himself honestly to his son; again, he backs away from real engagement with Paul and misses the chance to show him through *action* that self-reliance does not preclude the social and economic justice that can only come from people acting together.

So Frank walks off with his disappointed son. The walk turns out to be long. It ends in the historic baseball field of Doubleday Park, where they sit and watch middle-aged men dressed up in the uniforms of major league clubs playing baseball and having their pictures taken, certainly not what Paul has come to see. They talk, watching the uninteresting game before them. Frank tries to tell Paul that he shouldn't worry so much, shouldn't let so much 'get to him'. Paul answers, speaking of his adolescence, that these days everything seems to completely change in six-month cycles, to which his father replies that adults have other problems, like that their cycles 'last a lot longer', but rather than develop this conversation he ends it lest it 'send his [Paul's] mind off inventorizing Mr Toby [the dead hound], his dead brother, the electric chair, being fed arsenic, the gas chamber – on the hunt for something new and terrible in the world to be obsessed by and later make jokes about.' So another opportunity is lost.

On their way back to the Hall of Fame, they come to batting cages with coin-operated pitching machines. As with the basketball DIY machine, Frank insists he has to try it; Paul, he says, can coach. This suggests that Frank isn't going to insist that Paul try it, too. Each of the cages is signed with its pitching speed. Frank, of course, chooses the fastest, the one pitching at 75 miles per hour. He takes a bat but doesn't, as signage directs, put on a protective batting helmet, and he elaborately prepares to bat. Paul reminds him that they were supposed to do 'Something about a hall of fame?' Frank says they'll get there, adds 'Trust me.' He directs Paul to put the coins in and waits for the first of the five pitches to come. Frank does not do well. Paul does not coach well, making caustic comments. Frank turns from father into rival, saying 'Since you're the expert, you need to try it.' Paul, who has no intention of trying it, says, 'Right', sarcastically. Frank taunts his son while Paul photographs his father doing it. Paul eventually says, 'Fuck you', at which Frank finds 'pity and murder and love each crying for a time at bat', and he hugs and squeezes his son in a sort of tender wrestling hold which Paul struggles against, the two of them then really scuffling until Frank is at last embarrassed and lets go, finding that his arm around Paul's head has rubbed the bandage off Paul's cut ear. Frank sees 'beet-red blood down my middle finger and smeared in my palm'. He has to say something:

> *'All in fun. No big deal,' I say. I flash him a lame, hopeless grin. 'High fives.' One hand is up for a slap, the other, bloody, one finding my own pocket. Sunglassed tourists continue observing us from forty yards out in the parking lot.*
>
> *'Gimme the cocksucking bat,' Paul seethes and, ignoring my high fives, goes tramping past me, grabbing the blue bat off the fence, kicking the gate open and entering the cage like a man come to a task he's put off for a lifetime.*
>
> [...]

He suddenly turns back to me with a face of bright hatred, then looks at his toes again as if aligning them with something, the bat still sagging in spite of one attempt to keep it up. He is not a hitter to inspire fear. 'Put in the fucking money, Frank,' he shouts.

'Bat left, son,' I say. 'You're a southpaw, remember? And back off a little bit so you can get a swing at it.'

Paul gives me a second look, this time with an expression of darkest betrayal, almost a smile. 'Just put the money in,' he says. And I do. I drop two quarters in the hollow black box.

This time the green machine comes alive much more readily, as if I had previously wakened it, its red top light beaming dully in the sun. The whirring commences and again the whole assembly shudders, the plastic hopper vibrates and the rubber tires start instantly spinning at high speed. The first white pill exits its bin, tumbles down the metal chute, disappears then at once reappears, blistering across the plate and smacking the screen precisely where I'm standing so that I inch back, thoughtful of my fingers, though they're stuffed in my pockets.

Paul, of course, does not swing. He merely stands staring at the machine, his back to me, his bat still slung behind his head, heavy as a hoe. He is batting right-handed.

'Step back a bit, son,' I say again as the machine goes into its girdering second windup, humming and shuddering, and emits another blue darter just past Paul's belly, again thrashing the fence I'm now well back of. (He has, I believe, actually inched in closer.) 'Get your bat up to the hitting position,' I say. We have performed hitting rituals since he was five; in our yard, on playgrounds, at the Revolutionary War battlefield, in parks...

'How fast is it coming?' He says this not to me but to anyone, the machine, the fates that might assist him.

'Seventy-five,' I say. 'Ryne Duren threw a hundred. Spahn threw ninety. You can get a swing. Don't close your eyes (like I did).' I hear the steam organ playing: 'No use sit-ting a-lone on the shelf, life is a hol-i-day.'

The machine goes into its Rube Goldberg conniption. Paul leans over the plate this time, his bat still on his shoulder, gazing, I assume, at the crease where the ball will originate. Though just as it does, he sways an inch back and lets it thunder past and whop the screen again.

'Too close, Paul,' I say. 'That's too close, son. You're gonna brain yourself.'

'It's not that fast," he says, and makes a little eeeck and a grimace. The machine circuits then into its next-to-last motion. Paul, his bat on his shoulder, watches a moment, and then, to my surprise, takes a short ungainly step forward onto the plate and turns his face to the machine, which, having no brain, or heart, or forbearance, or fear, no experience but throwing, squeezes another ball through its dark warp, out through the sprightly air, and hits my son full in the face and knocks him flat down on his back with a terrible, loud thwack. After which everything changes.

In time that does not register as time but as a humming motor noise solid in my ear, I am past the metal gate onto the turf and beside him; it is as if I had begun before he was hit. Dropped to my knees, I grab his shoulder, which is squeezed tight, his elbows into his sides, both his hands at his face – covering his eyes, his nose, his cheek, his jaw, his chin – underneath all of which there is a long and almost continuous wheeee sound, a sound he makes bunched on the plate, a hard, knees-contracted bundle of fright and lightning pain centered where I can't see, though I want to, my hands busy but helpless and my heart sounding in my ears like a cannon, my scalp damp, airy with fear.

This scene at the batting cage is the turning moment. Frank himself says so in 'After which everything changes.' If you object that this is just another way of speaking of the novel's climax, you're of course right, in that it's the point in the plot of maximum conflict at which one or other of the forces producing the story conflict had to yield; the knight slaying the dragon or the dragon slaying the knight, or the anticlimax in which the man and beast become pals, etc. But here I mean a point of maximum conflict/tension which forces the beginning of a new self-knowledge in the protagonist which will change his or her behaviour, change the way the character *acts*, which should at least appeal to Frank Bascombe.

And the best of these turning moments involves a character who's been written so that you understand both the potential for such change *and* the aspects of character that could keep him from changing, or even make him change for the worse. With Frank, they're positive. He begins to realize his responsibility for Paul's 'accident' and, in retrospect, for some essential emotional neglect, even aversion, caused by his absorption with his own feelings of loss and abandonment subsequent to his divorce and his ex-wife's remarriage.

You're caught up in Boscombe's character and relationships because of Ford's superb ability to create social complexity with a lucidity that convinces you that the character's thoughts and feelings are presented so right and so accurately wrong.

When driving Paul between halls of fame, Frank, thinking how little he wants to be alone in the car with his son, does capture both his loss of adult responsibility and exactly the way any parent might for a time feel during a particularly obnoxious display of ignorant adolescent nastiness posing as 'grown-up' independence. Ford makes Paul become every middle-class, educated parent's worst nightmare of a son – foul-mouthed, tactless, mean, self-centred, argumentative, dull, geeky, with an attention span in nanoseconds. Not to mention irritating facial habits and weird ironic cries for help and barks coming on like nervous tics. And dirty and smelling bad.

One of Ford's great ideas of character building up to this turning moment is having Frank try to relate to Paul by adopting some of the traits he can't stand – the foul language, the compulsive punning – all of which, naturally, feed the anger Frank has to suppress. So we watch as one by one all of Frank's grand bonding plans – the fishing, the big meals, the halls of fame, the good old father–son talk about fine old Emerson and the truly excellent old Declaration – are aborted, forgotten in anger, modified into hitting on a tired waitress to unlock the kitchen for a plate of cold spaghetti. And beneath this, even more telling, is Frank's false assumption that Paul shares his own sporting interests. (Ann, the ex-wife but constant mother, knows this.) And yet Ford's writing, his placing of Paul's various bits of annoyance, shows this as Paul's plea for help, for Frank to relax (just as Frank says this to Paul) and just spend some ordinary time with him, not this fastball time on highways or in lectures posing as pal talk.

This is a fine turning moment in fiction because the action so encapsulates both Frank and Paul's struggles with independence and self-reliance, self-reliance for Paul being these adolescent experiments at self-assertion. Frank will show him how it's done.

He chooses the fastest pitching machine to bat against, ignores the instruction to wear the protective helmet, closes his eyes (closes his eyes!) when he swings, cannot manage a hit, and gets mad at Paul's genuinely witty heckles: 'Strike five, you're history!' and 'The Sultan of Squat'. This might have been the time when Frank could have laughed and praised his son's wit and way with words – but no.

The wrestling that should have been the hug Frank tells himself he really meant was another chance to wake up to his anger. But instead he forgets to insist that Paul wear the batting helmet. The scene begins, you note, much like Paul with the basketballs. It seems he's going to let all five pitches go by without taking a swing, that is, in another baseball term, without making contact. This connection reminds you that, as with the basketballs, Paul's real aim is to show his father that he is Paul, not his father's idea of Paul.

This is dramatically developed in Frank's dialogue, pitch after pitch. You already know he's batting from the wrong side. First, 'Step back a bit, son'; then, 'Get your bat up to the hitting position.' (Anyone who knows baseball at all would understand that batting wrong-handed to fast pitching is completely hopeless. Frank is living a fantasy here, calling instructions to someone who is not there.) Finally, after a pep talk about how really seventy-five isn't so fast, before the terrible fourth pitch, 'That's too close, son. You're going to brain yourself.' That he didn't stop Paul when he didn't bat left-handed from the start is bad enough. That he doesn't start to interfere when he says Paul is literally at risk is awful.

Paul, in stepping on to the plate and facing full on to the machine, doesn't really want to get hit in the face. *He really wants his father to see him.* To see he's Paul, Paul.

Paul, whose eye is severely injured when he's hit, who will need an operation to save its sight, could well have been permanently damaged or even killed by the hard ball hitting him at high speed. But it's Frank, not Paul's, responsibility to act like an adult and to care for his son.

Ford gives you what you want, Paul living and not losing his eye but suffering enough for Frank to begin to change, and you feel that this moment has been so well prepared for both through the first four-fifths of the novel and so believable from this point for its last fifth that you haven't been aware of the craft of it. Which is the point, isn't it, of such a turning point?

Workshop

Look at some representative climaxes in your fiction. If you have a draft of a novel, include its climax in the workshop considerations below as well as those of short stories.

- How significant is the climax itself – its action – to the revelation of character?
- Does its revelation of character extend to more than one character?
- How have you constructed the character(s) prior to the climax so that the climax has significance in further revealing aspects of their character(s)?
- Does what happens after the climax (the denouement) make sense in terms of the climax and continue to develop character?
- Does the Carver story in the first part of this chapter have a turning moment as defined in the second part?

If any of your responses to the first four questions above has been negative, you should consider some revisions to the piece of fiction involved.

Remember that you learn to write better just as you learn to write – by writing.

Focus points

- 'Narrative voice' is the sound to your reading ear that communicates character, the 'living' person who tells you the story, their own or others'.
- A turning point in a story is where the character or characters involved must change and go in a new direction – yet one that is compatible with their earlier character development.

References

CHAPTER 1

Thomas Hardy, *The Return of the Native* (Macmillan, 1962).

Saul Bellow, *Humboldt's Gift* (Avon, 1975).

Martin Amis, *The Information* (Vintage, 2008).

Hilary Mantel, *Bring Up the Bodies* (Fourth Estate, 2012).

Cormac McCarthy, *All the Pretty Horses* (Knopf, 1992).

CHAPTER 2

E.M. Forster, *Aspects of the Novel* (Harvest Books, 1954).

Russian Fairy Tales, trans. Norbert Guterman (Pantheon Books, 1945).

Flannery O'Connor, 'The Comforts of Home', *Everything That Rises Must Converge* (Noonday Press, 1966); *The Violent Bear It Away*, in *3 by Flannery O'Connor* (Signet, 1962).

James Joyce, 'Clay', *The Essential James Joyce* (Cape, 1948).

Malcolm Lowry, *Under the Volcano* (Penguin Modern Classics, 1963).

Irving Weinman, *Virgil's Ghost* (Fawcett Columbine, 1989).

CHAPTER 3

Alison Lurie, *Truth and Consequences* (Chatto & Windus, 2005).

Claire Messud, *The Woman Upstairs* (Virago, 2013).

Ralph Ellison, *Invisible Man* (Signet, 1952).

Fyodor Dostoyevsky, *Notes from Underground* (Oxford, 1994).

Henrik Ibsen, *A Doll's House*, in *Eleven Plays of Henrik Ibsen* (Modern Library, 1950).

Adam Johnson, 'Hurricanes Anonymous', in *Best American Short Stories 2009*, ed. Alice Sebold (Houghton Mifflin Harcourt, 2009).

Joy Williams, 'Taking Care', in *Taking Care* (Vintage, 1982).

CHAPTER 4

Joseph Conrad, *Heart of Darkness* (Norton Anthology of English Literature, vol. 2, 1974); 'The Tale', in *The Tale* (Hesperus Press, 2008).

D.H. Lawrence, 'Rocking Horse Winner', in *The Portable D.H. Lawrence* (Viking, 1947).

Kazuo Ishiguro, 'Crooner', in *Nocturnes* (Vintage, 2009).

Claire Messud, *The Woman Upstairs* (Virago, 2013).

Doris Lessing, 'To Room Nineteen', in *Modern British Short Stories*, ed. Malcolm Bradbury (Penguin, 1988).

Ernest Hemingway, *The Sun Also Rises* (Scribner's, 1970).

CHAPTER 5

Jack London, 'To Build a Fire', in *An Anthology of Famous American Short Stories*, ed. Burrel and Cerf (Modern Library, 1963).

James Ellroy, *L.A. Confidential* (Arrow, 1994); 'Afterword' (2006), in *The Black Dahlia* (Mysterious Press, 1987).

Jane Smiley, *A Thousand Acres* (Harper Perennial, 2004).

Émile Zola, *Germinal*, trans. E.A. Vizetelly (Dent, 1933).

Philip Roth, *The Human Stain* (Vintage, 2001); *American Pastoral* (Houghton Mifflin, 1997).

CHAPTER 6

Irving Weinman, *How to Write Dialogue in Fiction* (Hodder Education, 2012).

Daniel Defoe, *A Journal of the Plague Year* (Routledge, 1884).

Herman Melville, *Moby Dick* (Modern Library, 1982).

Ivy Compton-Burnett, *Parents and Children* (Gollancz, 1960).

Jorge Luis Borges, *Fictions* (Penguin, 1998).

Roberto Bolaño, *Nazi Literature in the Americas*, trans. Chris Andrews (Picador, 2010).

Kevin Powers, *The Yellow Birds* (Sceptre, 2012).

Ann Patchett, *Bel Canto* (Harper Perennial, 2008).

Iain Banks, *The Quarry* (Little Brown, 2013).

CHAPTER 7

Messud, *The Woman Upstairs* (Virago, 2013).

Shirley Jackson, 'The Lottery', in *Literature*, ed. Perrine (Harcourt Brace Jovanovich, 1978).

E.M. Forster, 'The Other Side of the Hedge', in *The Other Side of the Hedge; The Celestial Omnibus* (Kessinger Legacy Reprints, 2010).

William Golding, *Lord of the Flies* (Faber & Faber, 2005); *The Spire* (Harcourt, Brace & World, 1964).

Leo Tolstoy, 'How Much Land Does a Man Require?', in *Tales from Tolstoi* (L.C. Page 1901).

Cormac McCarthy, *Blood Meridian* (Vintage International, 1992).

Robert Coover, 'The Babysitter', in *Pricksongs & Descants* (Picador, 1973).

Sinclair Lewis, *Babbit* (Harcourt, Brace & World, 1901).

Don Delilo, *End Zone* (Picador, 2011).

Randall Jarrell, *Pictures from an Institution* (The Noonday Press, 1968).

CHAPTER 8

Raymond Carver, 'Where I'm Calling From', in *Cathedral* (Vintage Contemporaries, 1984).

Richard Ford, *Independence Day* (Vintage Contemporaries, 1996).

Index

action
    fast, 86–91
    short, 103–4
    slow, 83–6
    work as, 92–102
actors, 15
alcoholism, 159–60
All the Pretty Horses
    (McCarthy), 10–11
allegory, 135
American Pastoral
    (Roth), 101–2
Amis, Martin, 7–9
Austen, Jane, 9–10
autistic characters,
    122–31

Babbit (Lewis), 146
'Babysitter, The'
    (Coover), 146
Banks, Iain, 122–31
Bel Canto (Patchett),
    115–22
Bellow, Saul, 4–7
Blood Meridian
    (McCarthy),
    136–45
Bolano, Roberto, 110
Borges, Jorge Luis, 110

Call of the Wild, The
    (London), 165
Carver, Raymond,
    155–65
change in characters,
    33–41
Chesil Beach (McEwan),
    110
'Clay' (Joyce), 24–6
clichés, 49, 157

'Comforts of Home,
    The' (O'Connor),
    17–21
Compton-Burnett, Ivy,
    109–10
Conrad, Joseph, 57–62
context, 57–64
    in dialogue, 122–31
Coover, Robert, 146
'Crooner' (Ishiguro),
    65–9

Dante, 28–9
Defoe, Daniel, 107
DeLilo, Don, 149–52
depth of characters,
    16–30, 33–53, 135
dialogue
    context in, 122–31
    in descriptive
        narrative, 115–22
    extent, 109–11
    presentation, 107–9
    satire in, 149–52
    showing character,
        111–15, 123

Ellroy, James, 86–91
emotions, 47–9
End Zone (Delilo),
    149–52

fairy tales, 16–17
Fictions (Borges), 110
first-person narration,
    70–2, 155–7
flat characters, 16–23,
    26–30, 135
    slightly rounded, 20,
        23–6

Ford, Richard, 166–76
Forster, E.M., 22, 135
framing device, 61–2

Germinal (Zola), 94–9

Hardy, Thomas, 2–3
Heart of Darkness
    (Conrad), 57–62
Hemingway, Ernest,
    80
'How Much Land Does
    a Man Require?'
    (Tolstoy), 135
Human Stain, The
    (Roth), 99–100
Humboldt's Gift
    (Bellow), 4–7
humour, dark, 130–1
'Hurricanes Anonymous'
    (Johnson), 42–6

Independence Day
    (Ford), 166–76
Inferno (Dante),
    28–9
Information, The
    (Amis), 7–9
inspiration for
    characters, 3–12
interjections, 157
Ishiguro, Kazio, 65–9

Jackson, Shirley, 135
Jarrell, Randall, 146–9
Johnson, Adam, 42–6
*Journal of the Plague
    Year, A* (Defoe),
    107
Joyce, James, 24–6

L.A. Confidential (Ellroy), 86–91
language translations, 116–22
Lessing, Doris, 72–9
Lewis, Sinclair, 146
London, Jack, 83–6, 91, 164–5
'Lottery, The' (Jackson), 135
love, 48–9, 52–3, 67–9, 75–6
Lowry, Malcolm, 28
Lurie, Alison, 33–5, 38–40

Mantel, Hilary, 10
McCarthy, Cormac, 10–11, 136–45
McEwan, Ian, 110
Melville, Herman, 107–9
Messud, Claire, 36–41, 70–1, 134
Moby Dick (Melville), 107–9

naming of characters, 4–5, 9, 42
narrative context, 57–64
narrative viewpoint, 69–80
narrative voice, 155–66
narrator as character, 65–9
Nazi Literature in the Americas (Bolano), 110

O'Connor, Flannery, 17–22
openings
  capturing the reader, 40–1

detail in, 43
introducing character, 63–4
narration, 65–9
narrative voice, 155–7
'Other Side of the Hedge, The' (Forster), 135

parable, 135
Parents and Children (Compton-Burnett), 109–10
Patchett, Ann, 115–22
physical appearance, 24
Pictures from an Institution (Jarrell), 146–9
point of view, narrative, 69–80
Power, Kevin, 111–14

Quarry, The (Banks), 122–31

Return of the Native, The (Hardy), 2–3
Roth, Philip, 99–102
rounded characters, 42–53
change, 33–41
rounded flat characters, 20, 23–6

satire, 146–52
second-person narration, 79–80
sentimentality, 43–4
settings as sources of character, 9–11
short stories, rounded characters in, 42–53

Smiley, Jane, 92–3
social settings, 10–11
stereotypes, 23
Sun Also Rises, The (Hemingway), 80
symbolism, 134–45

'Taking Care' (Williams), 47–53
templates, other stories as, 28
third-person narration, 72–9
Thousand Acres, A (Smiley), 92–3
'To Build a Fire' (London), 83–6, 91, 164–5
'To Room Nineteen' (Lessing), 72–9
Tolstoy, Leo, 135
Truth and Consequences (Lurie), 33–5, 38–40
turning points, 166–77

viewpoint, narrative, 69–80
Virgil's Ghost (Weinman), 28–9
voice, 155–66

Weinman, Irving, 28–9
'Where I'm Calling From' (Carver), 155–65
Williams, Joy, 47–53
Woman Upstairs, The (Messud), 36–41, 70–1, 134

Yellow Birds, The (Power), 111–14

Zola, Émile, 94–9